Hidden Portals

To Supernatural Power

Jeanne Dann

PRESS

Hidden Portals
To Supernatural Power
by Jeanne Dann

Printed in the United States of America

ISBN 978-1-60647-625-3

www.xulonpress.com

Table of Contents

Preface

Although many of the events described in this book are actual experiences that different people have had at various times in their lives, it is not intended to be a biography of anyone's early years. As a fictional book, written in the first person, it is the intent of the author to bring you, the reader, into a relationship with the character, Selima Jeruelli, (pronounced Sa-LEE-ma Ja-ROO-lee) as though she is talking directly to you. Selima wishes for you, her new friend, to use your imagination as she takes you on a journey into the supernatural realm with her. There are things that she desires for you to experience along with her and these can be real and actual experiences for you.

I hope you will begin to connect with this character and the other characters in this book because there is no end to the supernatural things that can happen to you or them. Enter the world of the supernatural and change your life for it is a life of mystery and intrigue waiting to be discovered.

1

First of All

I wish my brother Jason had not gone over to Micah's house to spend the night or at least had remembered to take his cell phone with him. Maybe he forgot to charge it but all I know is I can't get a hold of him and I don't know Micah's number. He won't be back until sometime this afternoon and I'm *really desperate* to talk to him! I've got to share with him what happened last night. It was so incredible I can hardly contain myself!

I went to this place to hang out and there were so many things going on there. Get this! My whole body has been constantly vibrating ever since last night, kind of like strong shivering even though I'm not cold. I hardly got *any* sleep last night from all of the excitement and now it's almost two in the afternoon and I'm *still* shaking!

I've just been kicking back here on my bed thinking about it most of the day. My bedroom is decorated in lavender and lime green and it's really bright and cheery; so inviting with lots of fun throw pillows on the bed, a comfy bean bag chair covered in a soft velvety material in lavender over on one side, and a tall bookshelf full all my cool girl stuff, small collectables and good books. I could just spend hours in here and never get bored. My room and is on the second floor of our four-bedroom home and faces the east side. The fourth bedroom is reserved for when we have family or guests over to spend the night.

When I look out my bedroom window, I can see the neighborhood park and on a clear, sunny day - a beautiful view of Mount Rainier. Today though, all I can see are clouds blocking my view. It's been overcast and gloomy all day, which seems to be the usual weather for Washington State in November. But the weather doesn't really matter today because I feel like I'm about to explode with excitement just thinking about what happened last night!

Zoë was there with me and is the only one who could possibly understand what I'm feeling right now. She's so pretty and has a cute, petite figure and beautiful, shoulder length red hair and has been my very best friend since we first met in 6th grade. I could call or text-message her right now or send her a note on myspace, but I really feel like I'd rather talk to Jason about it. I need to apologize to him for not letting him know ahead of time about this event. He's going to be really upset with me when he finds out what he missed out on!

So anyway, my life took a dramatic turn almost two and a-half years ago. Before then, I couldn't have imagined that life could be such an exciting adventure. I don't think I would want to change a thing and *I will never go back to my old boring life again!* In fact, things have changed for me radically just since last night! But **first of all**, before I tell you more about that, let me catch you up on who I am.

Three months ago on August 7th, I turned 14. I live with Jason, who is one year older than me, and my parents, who met and married here in Washington after Mom moved up from California to go to Art school and afterwards, decided to stay.

We live in a gated community in a development outside of Meadow Bay. It's a quiet neighborhood where everyone's friendly and there's about 8-10 of us youth that live here, but we don't actually hang out that much, especially during the summer. We *do* talk at the bus stop in the morning before school, walk each other home from the bus after school and that's about it.

I'm currently in the 9th grade at Brightman Junior High. I have a small group of close friends there who I think are all really cool although we don't hang out with the "preppy crowd". They tell me that my best features are my big eyes, smile, and my thick hair. My friend Caryn is always telling me that I should to be a model but that's not exactly my personality. Besides, I don't think I'm *all that* pretty! In fact, models are supposed to be taller than I am – like 5 foot 8 or taller, I think. I'm about 5 feet, 6 inches and have blue-green eyes and long, brown hair.

One of my passions is reading so I like carrying a book around with me in case I have a spare moment.

I enjoy all kinds of books like adventures, mysteries, detective stories, sometimes love stories, and an occasional biography. My friends and family call me a book fanatic. In my opinion, it's a lot more interesting visualizing what the words are describing than to have no imagination and watch everything on screen with nothing for the brain to do but just figure out the plot. I guess you can tell by now that I don't watch a ton of TV. The Discovery and History channels are informative and some of the scientific and detective investigating shows are interesting but there are really only a few shows that I like to watch. I guess I'd have to say that the shows I enjoy the most are reality and competition shows- like singing and dancing.

Music is another one of my passions. I could listen and hum or sing along with it for hours, especially if I'm engrossed in a good book. My ipod earphone is like a permanent fixture in my ear! Mom's constantly asking me how I can concentrate on reading or homework when my music is playing 24/7. Sometimes I just can't think without it! How about you – do you like listening to music? I also like playing my flute or the piano and expressing myself that way. I'm not too good in sports but I do enjoy working out and swimming at our local YMCA and just hanging out there with my friends.

Jason and I are pretty close. He's a sophomore at Silver Creek High School and he's fairly cute for a brother. He's got brown hair like mine and always wears it in different spiky gelled-up styles and he has nice blue-green eyes and a great smile. Now he is the one who should be a model! He's a cool big brother, who's protective of me, keeps my special secrets and cheers me up if I get down about something. We are constantly laughing and teasing each other and have always been best friends growing up.

He's not into competitive sports but he does go snowboarding in the winter with his friends, when there's snow in the mountains, and he likes going to the gym with me and his buddies. What he *is into* is music like me; only he's a super talented singer. He's scored really high marks at the state competitions and earned a spot in a very prestigious choir with other youth from 5 different North Western States! He was also chosen at his high school for an elite musical group that travels around to perform at local and national functions. That has kept him pretty busy this past year. He's been thinking about trying out for <u>American Idol</u> next year. He's also got a gift for designing and working with his hands, creating all kinds of cool stuff with wood and metals.

Summers are some of our best times together since we love spending time outdoors, and just hanging out with our close friends and cousins. We like camping up in the mountains or at different lakes or over at the coast where we can hike and swim. There are so many beautiful places to see here; all the lakes, ocean beaches, mountains and rivers! It's a pretty cool place to live, if you can put up with the rainy months.

Wait a minute! Oh my gosh, what is happening? Giggles are starting to fill up my insides like I've never felt before and now I'm exploding with laughter and it's becoming uncontrollable! I can't help myself from just rolling in laughter as I'm lying here on my pillow! *Wow, I just can't seem to stop the spontaneous laughter!* My stomach and my sides are starting to get a cramp, I'm laughing so hard!

Why am I laughing? *I don't even know what is so funny!* The laughter starts to slow down long enough for me to catch my breath but then it just starts back up again. It seems like there is some kind of force or power inside me doing all the laughing and I'm just going along for the ride. *I can't believe this!*

It's not even close to the same sound as my usual laughter; it is *way* louder and more vigorous! You know, there is something *really quite unusual* about this! I wonder if Zoë has ever had this happen to her. Have you ever had this happen to you, friend? It's actually kind of fun. I wish I could tell you what was so funny so that you could laugh along with me *but I just don't know!*

This reminds me of the youth retreat that I went to a little over two years ago, shortly before I turned 12, when those kids were on the floor laughing out of control. They were rolling back and forth; holding their stomachs like it was hurting. I wonder if they had this same kind of feeling. I'll have to ask Zoë if she knows anything about this. If anyone knows, she probably does because she has been around a lot of supernatural events in her life!

Sweet! Now this comforting feeling of warmth is coming all over me. It feels like warm honey pouring over my head and down over my entire body to my feet like being wrapping up in a nice warm blanket. I feel really peaceful now since that's happened to me and the laughter has finally calmed down along with the shaking from last night.

When I started thinking about the retreat that first weekend of summer vacation before Junior High started, my thoughts raced even farther back to the time when I first learned how to play the flute, since now I'm starting to see that all of these things are related to each other. Let me tell you about that time now, my friend.

My mom is a piano teacher and decided that I should learn music at a really early age. So when I was five, she started giving me piano lessons. But as I got older, she singled me out from her other students, giving me all these really difficult songs to learn and expecting way more from me than what I thought was fair. She was not a strict parent but when it came to piano, she had high expectations for me and wanted me to excel! However, she was *not* very good at making that happen without treating me quite rudely and often making me cry with her harshness! (Don't tell her I said that.)

Anyway, in the 4th grade I decided it was time for a change because of the tension that was growing between us. I think I learned a lesson from all that. It's not always wise to have a parent for a teacher; at least not when it comes to learning to play an instrument! So my solution to all this was to take band class at school to learn to play a different instrument. I chose the flute because all the reed instruments made my lips tickle from the vibration, and brass instruments just didn't fit my feminine side.

But, let me tell you, band class was one of **the** worst, most annoying classes I have ever set foot in! You have to be *so extremely patient* with everyone while they were learning to play their instrument! The sounds of the notes coming out of some of the instruments were *so horrible!* I'm sorry, but that's just the way it is! Not only that, but there were so many interruptions that it seemed like nothing *ever* got accomplished. Since I already knew how to read music, my musical abilities exceeded most of the beginners even though I didn't know how to play the flute very well yet.

But I was determined to learn a new instrument and take a break from learning the piano. Mrs. Shelby, the band teacher, knew that my mom gave me piano lessons and she had a great idea to give me private lessons. That turned out to be the *perfect* fit! I wouldn't have to be in that miserable band class anymore and I wouldn't have to take lessons from Mom either! I learned to play the flute quickly and discovered that I loved playing it, so my practice sessions were never boring and it gave me a sense of accomplishment. Mrs. Shelby was very kind and helpful as a teacher and she commented several times that I had a natural ability for the flute.

When she saw my potential, she arranged for me to join a music company in the community that toured and played before audiences with as many as 200 people. At first, the conductor put me in 3rd chair but immediately promoted me to 2nd chair. That's how you're classified within each instrument section and it determines which notes you play in the song.

There are mostly adults in this company and since I was only 9 years old at the time that I started, the conductor placing me immediately into the 2nd chair position stirred up quite a controversy!

I was honored by the confidence my conductor had in me but it hurt when I heard people were talking about me behind my back. I made up my mind that I was going to do my very best in spite of what other people thought. No matter what, I didn't want to let down my teacher since she was the one that made it all possible for me. I definitely couldn't quit over other people's jealousy and gossip!

I needed to get braces put on my teeth soon after I started this company and I had to learn to adjust to the new positioning of my teeth and lips on the mouth-piece. I continued playing in 2nd chair even though I had to work much harder to maintain the same sound quality. It just didn't come quite as naturally as before. Then, after my braces were taken off in the 6th grade, the struggle was over and I started playing extremely well. I'm not trying to brag although it sounds that way. That's when the conductor promoted me to first chair and what an honor that has been! That's when I had to start working hard to show I deserved to be there! I am still playing with this company now and there are just the *two of us* in first chair! We have 8 flutist altogether.

I'm really grateful for Mrs. Shelby and my conductor (and my mom, of course) for helping me to excel in my musical abilities. I was a little sad to leave elementary school, knowing I wouldn't be seeing Mrs. Shelby anymore. I decided not to take lessons from her anymore, since my conductor has now been continuing to train me and challenge me with ways to keep improving my tone quality and technique.

After recalling my early training on the flute, my thoughts have again strayed back to that first weekend right out of elementary school. Two weeks before that, Zoë informed me that her parents would pay my way if I would go with her to a youth retreat at Camp Sycamore.

I was a little cautious at first, since I hadn't ever been to a retreat before, but Zoë promised me that it would be lots of fun. She made sure to mention that I would need to bring my swimsuit along since there would be lots of fun water sports on the lake. Knowing that I loved swimming and water sports, I'm sure she knew that would be the deciding point to get me to say yes! She also made me promise to bring my flute too, but didn't explain why. My parents gave me permission to go and Zoë's parents made all of the arrangements.

As those two weeks passed, I started really looking forward to spending time out on the lake. I absolutely love the outdoors and I caught myself often daydreaming about how nice it would be to be lying out on an inflatable mattress on the lake as the water lapped the sides, and enjoying the warmth of the sun kissing my skin with an occasional cool breeze blowing past. I love getting tan, but my dad often gets on me for staying out in the sun too long. Ah, summer vacation was going to be so great! No more school, just relaxing with my ipod and a good book, and hanging out with Jason and my friends!

The weather that spring had been unusually warm for early June. The last week before school got out, it had gotten up to the mid 80's. The Saturday before the retreat, it rose to 89 degrees and for Washington with our higher humidity, that is *really hot!* If it stayed this warm and nice, it would be perfect weather for the retreat! Hopefully the cabins would be shaded and stay cool, though.

I couldn't wait to go swimming and lie out on the beach, with the possibility of hanging out with some new friends! I wondered who else was going and if there was anyone else that I knew besides Zoë's family. Zoë hadn't mentioned anyone but in any case, I was going to have a great time! Any place where there was a nice lake with water sports and nice weather was bound to be fun, right? Do you enjoy summers like I do, friend?

2

Destiny Discovered

School got out on Wednesday, June 15th and the retreat started on Friday at noon and lasted until Saturday evening. The events of those two short days have changed the direction of my life and will be forever stamped into my memory! Those days have not only changed *my* life, but have also changed the lives of many of my family members and other people we know as well.

I packed up all my things on Thursday and wondered all through the day what I was getting myself into. Zoë's parents, the Shepherds, picked me up about 11:00 the following morning, and we arrived at the camp just shortly before noon on the 17th. Zoë's sister, Becky, and her brother, Mark, came too. Her dad and mom were not there to be the retreat speakers, even though they are pastors, but had just come to be part of the chaperone team.

The weather had stayed fairly warm as I had hoped it would. When we arrived at the camp, it was shaded by many tall fir trees and the buildings looked rustic and inviting. The women's cabins were located on the opposite end of the retreat camp from the men's, so the guys dropped us off first and helped us carry in all of our belongings. Zoë's mom, Debra and Becky took two bottom bunks next to each other in our roomy cabin and Zoë and I took the top bunks above them. We unrolled our sleeping bags and laid them out on the bunk pads and got everything organized and ready for the night. Then we went to register and get our name tags before lunch, which was scheduled to be served at 12:30.

After lunch, there were several activities that had been arranged. For the water sports, they had water-skiing, wake-boarding, inner-tubing and jet-skiing. There was also a large gym with all kinds of in-door sports activities to enjoy. Everyone was required to sign up to use the facilities, so Zoë and I decided to sign up for water-skiing, since I had water-skied the summer before with my cousins, and Zoë had skied many times with her family.

The first available opening for two people to go out in the water-skiing boat was from 2:30-3:30 so we scheduled ourselves in for that time slot. After we finished eating, we changed into our swimsuits and went to hang out at the lake until it was time for us to ski. Zoë's family had brought a raft to enjoy on the water so we had Mark inflated it for us before he went off to the gym to find some guys to hang out with. Zoë, Becky and I floated out on the water together for a while after she introduced me to some of her friends from her church and a couple of others that she had met at other church events.

There was a girl named Suzanne who had really pretty long, thick blonde hair, one named Felicity with auburn hair and a very cute little laugh, and a guy named Steve whose good looks would certainly draw a crowd of girls. There were a few others but I don't recall their names now. They were all hanging out at the lake along with some other youth that Zoë apparently didn't know.

While we were out on the raft, Zoë let me know that there was a group of musicians who would be playing during the meetings. She begged me to think about the idea of playing my flute with them. She had previously found out that they would be meeting for a practice session at about 4:30 and insisted that I go to meet them. After a lot of urging, she convinced me to go. That gave us just enough time to water-ski, get back to the cabin, get showered and changed before going to the practice. We enjoyed our time in the sun and water and hanging with her friends before it was our turn to ski.

Becky decided to go over to the gym with Mark when the driver of the boat docked to let off the last group and pick us up. There were two others who had signed up to go out with us. We all found a place to sit and got our lifejackets on. Everyone was given about 15 minutes to be in the water.

A muscular looking guy named Brad was the first one to go and he chose to wake-board, which is kind of like snowboarding on the water. He was really experienced at it and showed off his skills with all kinds of tricks and jumps. I was almost convinced not to go out on the water *at all* after watching him steal the show! Next was a tanned girl named Liza, and she got up after the third try and skied almost three times around the lake.

Then it was my turn. On the second try, I got up but I couldn't get my knees to straighten up out of a deep knee bend so I just let go. But the next time I tried, I got right up and skied around the lake a little over two and a half times. I wasn't brave enough to try any cool tricks since I didn't want to fall and end my turn, so I just played it safe. But it was totally awesome to feel the cool breeze and fine mist blowing past my face and hair. It's *such* a great feeling to be skipping over the surface of the water at a fast pace, almost like flying! Friend, have you ever skied before? If not, you should definitely try it sometime if you get the chance. It is *so* exhilarating!

Zoë went last and she had no trouble getting right up. She's such a great skier that she looked like a professional out there! She's much better at sports than I am. She made it look extremely easy and toured the lake more than three times around. She looked so amazing with her striking red hair blowing back and her beautifully tanned body skimming across the water, crossing the boat wake with such style. Even though she was just a little over 12, her cute figure was getting the attention and cheers of all her friends on the beach as she skied past.

It was such a *great* afternoon and so much fun that I almost forgot about the whole "music thing". I felt a bit shy about going in there and blindly introducing myself and asking if they needed a flute player. Since I was not even 12 yet, I was sure they would just stare at me, smile and say, "Nice try kid, but maybe you need to come back in a couple of years when you're more experienced." But instead, they were all really friendly and made me feel totally comfortable. Later I learned that Zoë knew these guys all along and had told them all about me. She had planned this whole thing out ahead of time but left me in the dark on purpose so I wouldn't be opposed to her little idea.

My musical experience up to that point mostly consisted of playing by reading the notes, except for the times when I had memorized the music first. When I asked if they had music for the songs, they blankly stared at me, and shook their heads no. They had sheets of words to the songs with chords above the words, but no written music. That pretty well settled it, then. I just *couldn't* play with their group *without music to read!* I left there actually a little bit relieved. I was glad I didn't have to feel "put on the spot" or embarrassed for not knowing the material.

The evening meeting was scheduled for 7:00. During our tasty fried chicken dinner, the conversation mostly centered on the meeting and who the speaker was – which left me clueless since I didn't know the speaker or even what you do in a meeting. As everyone finished eating, they started gathering in the meeting hall, which was right next door to the cafeteria. I didn't know what to expect but I decided that it was probably going to be worth it if Zoë's family had offered to pay my way.

7:00 soon came and Zoë, a couple of her friends, and I had all gotten settled in our seats fairly close to the front on the right-hand side of the middle aisle. Zoë brought a notebook and pen to take notes and a small snack bag with gum and candy to munch on during the session. It all started when the musicians went up on the platform to play. Instead of using songbooks, they sang the lyrics to songs that were put up on the wall by an overhead projector.

This was all very new to me including the sound of the music. I had been to a church a few times where they used hymnbooks. But, this music was different, kind of happy and upbeat and more contemporary. This was nothing like any church music I had ever heard before. This was actually pretty nice. Everyone was smiling and clapping and a few even kind of danced a little bit in front of their seats.

After the first few energetic songs, the next ones got slower and softer and several of the youth were closing their eyes with their heads turned upwards and some were raising their hands up in the air. They all had peaceful smiles on their faces. It looked to me like they were expressing their feelings of love and appreciation to something or someone above them.

I stood with everyone else and tried to follow along with the words, even though I wasn't familiar with any of the songs. I clapped when they clapped but I wasn't so comfortable raising my hands in the air. Maybe it was just that I'd never done it and I didn't understand why they were doing it. I *did* close my eyes and take in the mood of the place as the soothing, uplifting music continued. I loved how my insides were feeling, kind of warm and happy. It was such a peaceful atmosphere to be in at that moment.

After the singing was over, a shorter man with spiky blonde hair and a kind face in his late thirty's or early forty's got up and talked for a while. I don't really remember what he talked about because I was daydreaming and also because I wasn't really relating with what he was talking about.

I just kept thinking about how the music sounded. Why had I never listened to this kind of music before? I wished I had known how to improvise instead of having to read music so that I could have played my flute with their group. It would have been fun to have joined in. I think I just might have found another favorite kind of music to listen to! I was curious if they had this kind of music in stores or on the internet that I could download onto my ipod. I definitely decided I wanted to get some of that music if it was available or downloadable. It just made me feel so good and the words were so uplifting!

After the speaker talked for awhile, he requested that everyone come forward to the front of the stage. I didn't quite understand what was going on because I really hadn't been paying too much attention. I followed Zoë up and stood beside her on her right. I looked over at her and we smiled at each other. I wondered what was going to happen next and why we were all standing up there. The group of musicians went back up on the stage and started playing that really soothing music again.

The speaker started on the left-hand side of the stage and went down the line, talking to each person.

I was shocked at what I saw and wondered what kind of powers he possessed because while he was talking to each one, the things he was saying or doing was *causing nearly everyone to fall backwards on the floor!*

Certainly he wasn't a big enough man to push everyone over, and besides, why would he do that? He would make people angry, especially youth, if he was pushing them over. But no one seemed too bothered by what he was doing. Some of the youth were crying or were completely still like they had fallen asleep while *others were laughing so hard, they seemed to be out of control!*

There were guys standing behind each one to catch them *as if they knew ahead of time that they were going to fall!* Wow, this was all really strange! What was going to happen when he got to me? Would I fall, too? I hoped not. Why was all that happening? What was he saying or doing? *Maybe he had some kind of trance powers or something!* But Zoë didn't seem too bothered by what he was doing and she came up here like all the rest. She would know if this was some kind of voodoo or something, I'm pretty sure!

When he got to Zoë, I tried to listen to what he was saying but the music seemed to be drowning out his words to her. All I knew was that I was next. I clasped my hands together and closed my eyes tightly and tried to stay calm. And then, it was *my* turn! I opened my eyes back up as he took both of my hands in his. He looked me straight in the eyes with this really kind, loving expression that could have melted me right into the floor. *So, maybe that was it, the others melted! Oh, that's impossible, Selima! There's no such thing!* Thoughts were quickly racing through my mind wondering what was going to happen next.

Then, he spoke these words to me very softly and kindly, "God has chosen you for a very special assignment and has given you a gift to play your flute before kings and very important people. The Lord will use you as a channel to open up "portals of power" and unlock people's hearts. You will play your flute as King David of old played his harp to calm people's fears. They will get healed of sicknesses and diseases and get free from depression and addictions to drugs and alcohol! He will do this for them if you will choose to play your flute for Him."

I was in shock at first and then tears began forming in the corners of my eyes. *Wait! Why was I tearing up? After that, my legs didn't work anymore* and *the next thing I knew, I was lying on the floor like all the others! I had no idea what had just happened or how I got on the floor without feeling a thing? That was so incredible!* I felt light as a feather and like I could have just floated off somewhere. I had this peaceful, warm sensation inside my stomach but at the same time, I had all these questions swirling around in my mind.

First of all, how was it possible for this man to know I played the flute? Zoë must have told him ahead of time because I had been with her all day and I hadn't seen her talk to him so I know she didn't tell him about it today.

Secondly, how did he know that I would be playing for important people and all that stuff about disease and drugs? What did he mean when he said I would play my flute for God? That seems like a really tall order. And not only that, but what kind of powers did he possess that caused almost everyone to fall backward on the floor? *How does a person do that just by talking to them? This was so unreal!*

Lastly, what did he mean by "portals of power"? Was it like those secret entranceways in video games that take you into special rooms where you find extra treasures and weapons and extra powers and keys and stuff like that? He said I would unlock people's hearts. It seems like you would have to have some kind of special powers or keys or something to unlock people's hearts!

I looked over at Zoë and she was also lying on the floor like me. She had her eyes closed and was speaking in a language that I didn't understand. *She never told me that her family spoke another language!* It wasn't French, Spanish or German; I would have recognized them. Did she do some traveling that I didn't know about? Even more interesting to me was why she was choosing to talk in this language *now* instead of English. Maybe she didn't want anyone to know what she was saying. That must be the reason. But, wait a minute! She could also just talk to herself in her mind. Why was she talking to herself out loud? I've never seen her talk to herself!

I could hardly wait to discuss everything with her! I definitely had several things to discuss with her and many questions that needed answers! I was extremely excited and confused all at the same time. I felt so light and peaceful lying on the floor that I wasn't about to move for anything; not even if I *did* have questions.

As I continued to lie there, all my past flashed through my mind. *Had I just **discovered** my **destiny?*** Is this why I had learned to play the flute so fast and easily? If what that man said was true, then things in my life were beginning to make much more sense. I had *a reason and a purpose* for being on this earth and it was no accident that I had learned to play the flute! Wow, that's an awesome thought! But how could I possibly play my flute for God and how would I be given the opportunity to play for an audience of kings and very important people?

I hoped that what the speaker said *was actually true!* I have never had anyone tell me something about me or my future that I didn't already know myself. It was all quite mysterious. When I finally did get up off of the floor, I felt like I was still floating instead of walking. I felt kind of light-headed and maybe what some people must feel like after they had too much alcohol to drink or something like that.

This whole experience made me really glad that Zoë's parents had been so thoughtful to pay my way so I could attend this retreat. I have to be sure to remember to thank them since it was such a nice gesture! So far it's been just so *"way cool"!* I couldn't have had these experiences otherwise and I felt so refreshed!

I didn't know anyone who could tell you about your future except for psychics but he seemed to know all about my flute playing. Maybe *he is a psychic* or else he must have a pretty good memory if Zoë told him about my flute playing some other time. It just didn't seem like Zoë or her family to go listen to a psychic. Well, that's just another question to ask her.

3

Encoded Language

We were served hot chocolate, cookies and lots of other treats after everyone had gotten up and started to hang out. Then, it was time to head to our cabins for the night. I was totally glad for that. By now, I was *so* ready to talk to Zoë. I quickly changed into my night shirt and climbed up on my bunk.

"Hurry, Zoë! We have to talk!" I pleaded. When we were all snuggled up in our sleeping bags, I began by asking her if she had previously told the speaker that I played the flute. She insisted she had not and asked me why I wanted to know.

That's when I told her everything he had said to me word for word. I remembered it like I had recorded it - which I really had! It was forever burned into my memory files! I couldn't seem to erase the words from my thoughts. It was like the repeat button was on and it kept playing "portals of power", "playing your flute for kings", "unlocking people's hearts", "if you will play your flute for Him", over and over in my mind!

Zoë then told me that it was the Lord that had communicated to him those things about me. She made it very clear that the speaker, Elder Jeff, was *not* using psychic powers but instead, was listening to the voice of God talking to his human spirit. She told me that it's a powerful gift that the Lord gives people to know things about people that only God knows, since God knows everything about us including our every thought. Zoë called it a 'word of knowledge' or prophecy or something like that.

It's such an indescribable feeling to know that God has talked to you personally through someone who could actually hear **His** voice. Wow, what a totally awesome concept to think that God knows me personally and said something personal to *ME, Selima Jeruelli!* Has God ever talked to you, my friend? Or has someone told you something that God told them to tell you? I'm very interested to know more about that powerful gift that God gave him. When he mentioned the thing about "portals of power," I wondered if hearing God's voice was one of those kinds of "powers" that comes through the "portals".

I decided that if God had told him about my flute playing, He must have told him those other things, too. I guess that would be logical to assume. It was just *so incredible and fantastic to believe!* How does a person hear God talking to them when He's clear up in heaven somewhere? How could that speaker know the difference between God's words and his own thoughts? He seemed to be *quite sure* of himself when he spoke it out. So, who was I to doubt it when he got the part about me playing a flute right?

I lay quietly for a while just contemplating the events of the day; skiing and all the fun we had on the lake in the sun, the new people I met, the meeting and the new music, everyone mysteriously falling on the floor, what the speaker said to me, so many things happening and so much to think about.

Everything was getting pretty quiet in the cabin now and most everyone was in their bunk beds. A couple of girls were preparing their skin and hair for the night. The only other noises now were a few creaks and squeaks from the bunks and the sound of quiet voices as old friends caught up while new friends got acquainted.

After thinking it all over, I still had many more questions than I had answers. When I looked back over at Zoë, she was looking up at the ceiling and was very still. It looked like she was talking to herself in that *foreign language* again.

"*Hey, Girlie*, I didn't know your family spoke another language," I said to her more quietly now. "Did you live in a foreign country for a while or something? I don't remember you telling me you spoke in a foreign language!"

"*Oh no, Selima!*" she replied back, also in a very soft voice, "We haven't lived in another country, but we are planning to go to a special place. I'm speaking in my native language of heaven. You see, someday I'm going to be with my Father where heaven will be my home and He gave me a supernatural heavenly language to speak to Him with while I'm still on earth. It's like an ***encoded language*** just between Him and I. He gives me words to say in His encoded language because I'm not always sure how to express myself to Him and sometimes I just don't know what to say while I'm praying. I speak the words out and He gives me words to say through my spirit."

"What, you're really not making much sense! How does He give you words to say? And besides, aren't you *afraid* to speak words out when you don't know what you're saying?" I insisted. "What if you're *cursing someone* or something like *that?"*

"Oh, that could never happen." she quickly replied back. "Holy Spirit gives this encoded language to you *completely for your benefit* and He will *only speak good things* through you to build up your spirit or pray through you to help someone else that only *He* knows the details about. You don't have to study to know this language because it's a free gift and, believe me; you *never have to be afraid of what you are saying!"*

"It's really kind of exciting to be God's partner in that way because one day when we get to heaven, He's going to tell us about all the times when we helped someone else out by praying with our special language. This is such an exciting life when you know you have a destiny and a purpose."

"You see, we have an enemy in this world called satan who doesn't want us to give ourselves in service to the Lord or communicate with Him. He does all his activity in the unseen or spirit realm. He and his cohorts (his evil helpers) have the ability to suggest thoughts for us to think. But the enemy can't interrupt our thoughts to plant his ideas and evil suggestions into our mind while Holy Spirit is praying through us, because this special language doesn't come from our mind. Because we speak it out from our spirit, it makes this the most pure and supernatural language there is!"

"You know, Selima, you can have your own encoded language too, if you make Jesus, God's Son, your Lord and Spiritual Guide. He wants for you to be part of His heavenly family because He loves you so much and He desires for you to have His language more than you could ever want it so that He can talk to you and through you and teach you about Himself! Is it okay if I tell you a little more about the Heavenly Father and His Son?" she asked.

"Oh, yeah sure, Zoë. Go ahead." I answered. "This is interesting. I haven't heard of any of this stuff before."

"You see," she continued, "when God made Adam and Eve and put them in the Garden of Eden, He gave them authority over the earth and everything in it. But He told them not to eat the fruit off of one of the trees called the Tree of the Knowledge of Good and Evil."

"Now, satan came to them in the form of a snake and lured them into eating the forbidden fruit instead of listening to God. By that choice of disobedience against God's instructions, they brought sin into this world. At that point, Adam and Eve lost their legal authority over the earth and the devil, satan, took it over. Now, everyone born since Adam and Eve has been born a sinner because of our ancestry back to them."

"God is so holy that He wasn't able to have a relationship with the people He created, because sin had separated us from Him. But God couldn't leave us in that separated state because He designed us to have a loving relationship with Him. God also knew ahead of time that Adam would fall from his position of authority, but He already had a plan."

"God sent His Son, Jesus, from His position of authority in heaven to be born on earth as a human. His mother had to be a virgin so that instead of a *man* being the father (because of the sin that's passed down); *God* could then be His Father. Jesus needed to live His life completely without sinning and by doing that, He could pay the penalty for *our* sin, and take back the authority that the devil had stolen from mankind."

"I know this all sounds a little much but the more you know, the more information you'll have to make an intelligent decision if you choose to serve Jesus as your Lord," she continued in almost a whisper now. "When He was nailed to the cross, He paid the very highest price, His life, to take away the sin that was in the world."

"In the Garden of Eden, after Adam and Eve sinned, an animal had to be sacrificed and the animal's skin was used to cover their nakedness (or their sin). Now, just by accepting the blood sacrifice of Jesus, we can have a covering for *our* sins, too. Jesus became that sacrifice that covers us."

"If we *truly believe* in our hearts that Jesus, by dying on the cross, provided full payment for our sins; then, we can become our Heavenly Father's sons and daughters and start having communication with Him again. He loves us so very much and is just waiting to receive His family back so that He can talk with us again like He did with Adam and Eve in the Garden."

"When Jesus rose from the dead and returned to be with the Father in heaven again, He sent Holy Spirit to teach us and be our guide to help us to understand these things. He was sent here in Jesus' place because He can be everywhere at the same time, which is called 'Omni-presence.' God also sent us a love letter through men hearing His voice- the Bible that tells us all about these things."

"As we accept the price Jesus paid, ask Him to forgive and cleanse us and make Him our Lord, He gives us a new start on life by transforming us. Then, we begin following what He wants us to do with our lives by Holy Spirit leading us and being our Guide. It's really quite simple. In fact, it's so simple that most people miss it or don't understand it."

"By the way, what Elder Jeff said to you tonight is God's personal invitation to you to follow Him because He's got great plans for you. The gift God gave you to play the flute is because He loves you so much. If you make Jesus your Lord, He will send His Holy Spirit Guide to live inside you. He can then use you and play through you to touch the kings and other important people He wants to draw back to Himself. He wants everyone to know He loves us so much and has already paid the price which was the penalty for our sins and He wants to receive us back into His forever family. So, does any of this make sense to you or have I totally lost you?" she inquired softly. "You're awfully quiet. Did I put you to sleep?"

"Oh no, my special friend," I whispered back, "I'm not asleep. I have heard every word. You are really quite knowledgeable about all of this. It must be really special to be a pastor's daughter and learn all about this first hand from your parents. It's just that I have so much to think about, my head is spinning. I just need a little quiet time to sort this all out in my mind. You don't mind, do you?"

"Of course not," Zoë whispered. "You take all the time you need. I totally understand. I know it was a lot to tell you about all at once. Forgive me if I'm a little bit too deep and heady."

"Oh no, you're fine," I replied back. "I have had a very interesting and full day. There have been so many new experiences today that I've never had before. I'll talk to you more in a little bit when I can sort some of this out. You can go back to your encoded language if you want. I'm sorry I interrupted you before. I didn't know *you were praying.*"

"Don't mention it. I'm glad we had this talk. I'll talk to you in a little while. I just hope I didn't get you too confused."

"Not at all," I replied back. "No one has ever taken the time to tell me any of this. It was quite informative."

4

First Portal

I lay quietly for a long while, thinking about all that she had said and all that I had learned and experienced that day. It was all so overwhelming and it took time to sort out my many thoughts.

I knew there was a God, but I guess I assumed that I had to be *good* enough and if I did everything just right, then when I died, I might earn the privilege to live with God in heaven. Am I the *only* one who had ever thought that? Mom and Dad never took us to church to learn about God and actually, we've really never had a conversation about Him. I'm sure glad I have a friend who was thoughtful enough to take the time to tell me the truth about Him.

I didn't know that everyone was born a sinner since Adam and Eve, and that Jesus took the penalty away for my sins and everyone else's when He died on the cross. I just thought there were some good people, like Zoë, and some who weren't so good.

I also didn't know God loved me so very much. I always thought that He was a Judgmental God and it took a lot to make Him love me or be happy with me or anyone else. I'm sure there are others like me who have thought this way. I can't be the only one.

Zoë is right, it did seem almost *too* easy – that the only things necessary for me to be in His forever family was just to believe what He did for me, ask for forgiveness for my past, and then just begin to follow Him. I wonder if I could really know that for sure. I guess the best way to find out is just to try it and see what happens. So here goes.

"God in heaven, if what Zoë said about You and Your Son Jesus is true, then I want Jesus to be *my* Lord, too. I want to learn all about You. Please forgive me for all the things I've done in the past that have kept You and me apart and kept me from wanting to know more about You and be close to You. I *really* want to be in Your "forever family"."

"Right now, I'm making the choice to not do things my own way anymore. I really need your help to show me the life You have planned for me to live. I want Holy Spirit to come to live inside me and make my spirit come alive and become my Teacher and Guide. Please give me that encoded language that Zoë talked about, so that we can talk together. I also want to play my flute for You and whoever You want me to play for. Amen"

Oh, my friend, do you know what happened after I made those few statements to *the God of the whole universe?* Let me just inform you that *instantly* my body got really hot and it felt like my whole insides were going to burst like some kind of fireworks were going off inside me or something. All my emotions were magnified and I felt more alive than I had ever felt in my life!

Then, right after that I felt like this cool breeze blow over me. It was like I had so much peace and love and happiness welling up inside. I was just so excited and happy, I wanted to laugh and scream and jump and cry all at the same time. It was so awesome that I'm even having a difficult time describing to you how great it was. What I didn't know until later was that it was because Holy Spirit *had* come to live in me and make my spirit come alive, that I was having all those heightened emotions and feelings.

Everything in the cabin was quiet except for some heavy breathers who had already fallen into a deep sleep (and a few snorers). The lights had already been turned off but I wanted to leap up, turn on the lights and shout at the top of my lungs and tell everyone in the world what was I was feeling.

Right at that moment it seemed like words were coming up out of my insides and I just had to speak them out. I'd never heard these words before. *Oh, sweet! I'm speaking in my new encoded language from Holy Spirit!* It was from that wonderful moment on, that I would come to know Holy Spirit more and more as He has become my closest friend, since He's always right here with me.

I didn't know it at the time, my friend, but those few statements to the God of Heaven and Earth were the simplest but most *profound, life-changing* statements that I could ever make in my entire life! I was so caught up in the moment that all I could think about was how great and wonderful I was feeling. I felt so clean and light like a big weight had been lifted off of me.

When I simply gave my life over to be guided by Holy Spirit, Jesus became the Lord and Savior of my soul. You can make the decision to do the same thing right now, too. This, my friend, is *the first and most important and special of the many "secret" or "hidden portals"* that you can enter into the supernatural realm. This takes you into the spirit realm *headed in the right direction.*

The supernatural can only be tapped into if you enter into the spiritual unseen realm. Any other passageway or portal besides following Holy Spirit will lead you straight through a portal into the enemy's territory where there is only disaster and heartache waiting for you.

You see, my friend, satan's motives and tactics are always masked in lies and deception and his only mission is to kill, steal, and destroy anything and anyone in any way he can. You see, his final end will be torment and suffering forever and he goes to any length to subtly deceive everyone he can to turn against God and join him in that horrifying place. He is the one that makes you have all kinds of fears, tormenting thoughts, and nightmares.

Worst of all is if you're following in his direction, you won't be able to know what true peace is! Only God's Spirit can give you peace. By entering the wrong way into the spirit realm, the enemy will let you experience the supernatural all right. But, when he's set the trap and you have taken the bait, you don't always know what you have done or even how to escape the place of torment that he can take you to.

What some people think is innocent and fun to do and doesn't think is a really big deal, can be *a very big deal!* Such things as séances, reading tarot cards, seeking out psychics to get "readings" over the phone, on-line or on television shows, or playing sorcery related games or even some card games and video and internet games, are actually *very serious* advances into satan's territory. Even watching horror movies can be an open door for the enemy to come in to torment you!

If you have already been experiencing fears that you can't get rid of, then possibly you have knowingly or unknowingly accepted something that the enemy had to offer and he is harassing you in your thoughts. Those feelings and thoughts come from the devil, and his very nature is to be sneaky and underhanded and tempt you to take his thoughts as your own. He doesn't play fair and he wants you to be ignorant and blinded of his evil ways and blinded from getting to know Jesus.

If you choose to follow Jesus, *He* will start opening your eyes to see how the devil operates. It's called prayer when you talk to God, but I'd rather just think of it as "talking to God," period. If you just speak to Him like He's right there with you (which He is) and you tell Him the simple things that I just said to Him but in your own words and from your heart, He can change your life forever just like He did for me.

If you enter through this **first portal** into the supernatural realm *the right way*, you are on your way to experiencing the most wonderful peace and happiness and love like nothing you've ever felt before! Your Father in Heaven, who is a Holy God, has not been able to communicate with you how much He loves you because of the sin nature passed down from Adam, which has separated you from Him. But, if you ask Him to forgive you for your past, (and/or present) and if you make Jesus your Lord, He will send Holy Spirit to come to you right at this very moment and be your Guide. Yes, the Creator of the Universe wants to fill your heart with His love right now if you ask Him!

Jesus died on the cross for all of us, and it's all because He was resurrected from the dead, and was victorious over what the enemy had to offer Him, that we can experience His peace and hope. Everyone is born with a body, a soul, and a spirit but because we live out of our feelings and our mind, which is called our soul, then our spirit is "dormant" or unused inside us until God awakens it by His Spirit.

You will find that your Father in Heaven has been very patiently waiting and anticipating the moment when you would choose to be forgiven and want to talk to Him. And you can get to know Him even better when you read the "Love Letter" He wrote to you, the Bible, and ask Holy Spirit to teach you how to understand it. You will discover *a whole new world* and life you never knew could be possible before now!

I will also tell you that this doesn't mean you'll never have another problem in your life. In fact, because the enemy doesn't like you choosing to follow God, things might become harder at first because you're in a fight for your eternal life. But you can experience a special peace and joy that the enemy can't take away, even *through* struggles you may encounter in life. I hope you will stop reading long enough to talk to God right now. He's been waiting to talk to you.

Okay, so now I'm getting back to that memorable night that has forever determined my destiny. "Zoë, Zoë, are you still awake?" I whispered. There was no answer. I leaned over my bunk to get a closer look at her but she had already fallen sound asleep. I didn't want to wake her, but at the same time I felt compelled to. *I needed to talk to someone!*

It was then that I missed Jason and wished that he had come too, so that I could have shared this night with him as well. I wondered what that speaker would have said to him. *Oh, my gosh!* I didn't even ask Zoë what he had said to her. I was so selfish and wrapped up with my own self that I didn't even bother to ask what he told her. How *rude* I was. I'll have to ask her tomorrow now and I definitely need to apologize.

Just at that moment, those foreign words started coming so fast that I could barely whisper them out fast enough. I spent the next while talking to my Heavenly Father in this new supernatural language

He had given me to communicate with Him, and I felt like I was floating, similar to how I felt earlier that night in the meeting room on the floor.

It was such a beautiful, peaceful moment and I felt so clean and refreshed and I had all this new love for my Heavenly Father and my Lord Jesus. *What a supernatural night!* That afternoon, I was having a nice time in the sun and water and by nighttime, I felt like a new person experiencing all those new and wonderful thoughts and feelings and having all those supernatural things happening to me! How could all that be possible in only one day?

5

Such a Happy Day

I really didn't know how long I was lying there whispering my new supernatural language but the next thing I knew, I was awakened by voices in the room. There was this "glow" surrounding me like I was looking out of brightly tinted sunglasses.

A peace and warmth had filled my insides and I was sure I was the happiest person in the whole wide world. As I looked around the cabin at the other girls who had come to the retreat, I felt like I loved them all deeply, even though most of them I hadn't even met yet.

I looked over at Zoë's bunk. *Zoë! Where was she?* I needed to talk to her about last night. I looked down at the beds below but her sister and mother were also gone. Just then, a voice rang out, "Breakfast in ten minutes!" Well, there was no time to talk with Zoë now.

"Has anyone seen Zoë?" I called out.

"I think I heard her slip out of the cabin nearly an hour ago," someone answered.

Oh, great! I was still in my sleeping bag and night shirt and I had to be ready in ten minutes? I gasped under my breath, "No way!" I would never be ready in time! I leaped off my bunk, threw on the clothes I had brought to wear that day, gathered up my brush and toothbrush and paste and ran to the restroom. It was in a separate cabin 15 -20 yards away. Hurriedly, I made myself presentable, rushed back to the cabin to put my stuff away, and raced across to the Cafeteria building.

Everyone had already left the cabin when I got back and I *really* didn't want to be last in line for breakfast! I hardly knew anyone, other than Zoë's family, and I didn't even know where they were. It wasn't like Zoë to leave me alone with strangers. But actually, this particular day was different in that all those girls in our rustic, homey cabin seemed more like my family *than my own family!* There was an intimate connection with them that I'd never felt with people before. Yes, I loved my own family, but this was different! What I later discovered was that now that I had been born into the family of God, these people were members of my forever family.

This new love in my heart for these people put a *huge* smile on my face. I got in line and got my food, then scanned the room looking for Zoë or her family. Seeing that I looked a little disoriented, a "preppie" looking girl came up to me, and took me by the hand. It was someone I had seen in our cabin this morning.

She said to me, "Hi, I'm Melissa. Come sit at our table. You came with Zoë, right?"

"Yah, thanks. I'm Selima."

"I'm glad you were able to come. Zoë said she was bringing a friend from school. Hey, guys, this is Selima, Zoë's friend." Everyone at the table greeted me. They all had their nametags on, which was great because I didn't have to remember everyone's name, since that's not one of my strong points.

Just then, Zoë walked up with a pitcher of juice. *"Oh, Selima!"* she gasped, "I'm *so sorry* I forgot to tell you last night that my family volunteered for breakfast duty for this morning weeks ago. I would have told you this morning but you seemed to be enjoying your sleep a little too much to be disturbed so I let you sleep in. I'll come and find you when I'm through here. Did you want some juice?"

"Sure, thanks. I've *got* to talk to you, Zoë. Hurry, Okay?"

"Yah, I'll try to hurry; there shouldn't be that much more for me to do now. So what's up? You look really happy about something. Did you call home and get some really great news or something?"

"No, but I'll tell you about it later. What is the schedule for this morning?"

"The meeting next door begins at 10:30, so we'll have some time to talk before it starts. Looks like you're in good company. You guys take good care of her while I'm working, *ya hear!*" She flashed her pretty smile and walked away.

"Of course we will." Melissa spoke up. "Selima, have you always lived in this area?"

"Uh-huh, up until I was 4, we lived on the North Side of Pacifica, and then we moved to Universal Palace. Then, the summer before 3rd grade, we moved out to the Summerset area. I met Zoë halfway through the 6th grade at Augusta Elementary and we've been friends ever since. She's such a sweetheart."

The girl across the table spoke up. She was also from our cabin. Her nametag said "Stephanie" on it. "So, what has happened to you? You've been wearing this really big grin on your face ever since I saw you in the cabin this morning. I don't recall you being this smiley and happy in the service last night. Was it something Elder Jeff said to you?"

"So, it's *that* obvious?" I asked. Emotions flooded my mind and tears began to form in the corners of my eyes. Oh, there was so much to tell, but I really wanted Zoë to be the first to hear the news and then, I wanted to tell the whole world!

How was I going to respond to these inquiring faces? Was I going to expose the secrets of my heart? Before I could think about what I was going to say, I heard myself exclaim, *"I made Jesus my Lord last night and I feel so happy inside, I can barely contain myself!"*

"Oh, that's totally excellent!" Melissa exclaimed. *"Selima, we're so happy for you and welcome to the family of God!* Does Zoë know yet?"

"No, I haven't had a chance to talk to her about it since last night before I made my decision. I'm telling you, this is **such a happy day**, I could just scream and dance and cry! Every kind of emotion that I'm not used to feeling has been filling my insides. And,

I feel like I've known you guys forever and we just met. How is all this possible since just last night?"

Stephanie reached out and gently took me by the hand, smiled and said, "Holy Spirit has placed the love of our Heavenly Father in your heart supernaturally. He has given you His peace and joy. There's a verse in the Bible that says, "The kingdom of God is righteousness, peace and joy in the Holy Spirit." You are now part of the kingdom of God so you are starting to enjoy the benefits of the Holy Spirit giving you new life."

"Now that you are a part of God's family, you will experience more and more what it means to live in this new kingdom. Yesterday, even though you didn't know it, you were still a member of the kingdom of darkness where satan rules, but now you are in the kingdom of light where our King Jesus rules and reigns. That's why your face is beaming with His peace and joy. You are radiating the light and love of God, which is one of the signs of His glory on you!"

"Oh, there is so much to learn!" I exclaimed. "How will I ever learn all this stuff? It's all so new to me!"

Stephanie continued, "Holy Spirit will teach you and show you things that you wouldn't have learned otherwise. The Bible will come alive for you now. What you would have read before may not have made any sense because your spirit was not yet revived. But now you can ask Holy Spirit whenever you have a question about the Word and He will make it clearer. And find a good church where they teach you the truth and help you until you get more familiar with everything. Zoë's dad's church is great."

Just then Zoë walked up. "What's goin' on, guys?" she inquired. With that, everyone else jumped up from the table, pushed their chairs in and excused themselves. "Hey, wait a minute! Do I have bad breath or body odor this morning or something? Why is everyone leaving just when I walk up?"

"We're going to take a walk down to the lake and we'll be back for the meeting. Besides, you two have some catching up to do." Melissa replied.

Zoë's eyes got really big. "*We do?*" she gulped. "*What is up, here?* Why do I feel like I'm the last to get in on all the good stuff? *What is everyone hiding from me?*"

"It's okay," I assured her. "But they're right; I do have something really important I have to talk to you about. Let's head over to our cabin and hopefully we can have a little privacy there."

"Great, we are alone! Now what is all this about and why do you seem so happy?" she demanded as she flung herself up onto her squeaky bunk when we got into our comfy cabin.

I climbed up and sat crossed-legged at the foot of her bunk, beaming with happiness. "*I made Jesus my Lord last night after you talked to me!*" I blurted out.

Tears of joy filled Zoë's eyes as she leaned forward to give me a long and loving hug. "*Oh Selima, that is so fabulous! I'm so happy!* God is so good to keep His Word. Welcome to the family! Now we will *forever* be sisters!"

"That's almost the same thing that the girls at breakfast said to me, that I was part of the family now. I just couldn't keep it a secret because I was smiling so much. My cheeks are starting to ache I've been smiling for so long; actually ever since I woke up. I'm so amazed at how differently I feel from yesterday to today. I have so much peace and joy in my heart that it's hard to describe. I also have to tell you that I received Holy Spirit's encoded language like you have. I whispered it out for a long time last night. I feel like I'm a totally different person than I was just yesterday!"

"You are!" she exclaimed. "The Bible says we become "new creatures" where all things have past and new things have begun. Many things in life will begin to take on new meaning and you will know and understand things that you never knew before."

"A really important thing to know right now is to always keep short accounts with God. By that, I mean that Holy Spirit is going to start teaching you things that He *wants* you to do or not do because He is changing your way of thinking to be like His. If you feel in your heart that something is disturbing, a lot of times that is Holy Spirit speaking to your heart to change that way of thinking or doing things."

"An example of that would be if one of your friends did something really mean to you, you might have wanted to get back at them in the past, but now Holy Spirit might nudge your spirit to forgive them and let it go. Or if you were thinking of taking some-thing that wasn't yours, He might make your spirit upset to let you know that He doesn't want you to do that."

"He uses your conscience to tell you when He's not pleased with something you are doing or thinking. But, He is so loving and gentle that you just *want to change it* to please Him. When you ask God to forgive you, He immediately forgives and cleanses you. Then your peace is restored and you'll be right back to how you feel right now. That is what I mean about keeping 'short accounts'."

"If you hold onto something for days and don't get it right with the Lord, you can start feeling under pressure or miserable and uncomfortable. That's when you know that you have separated yourself from the Lord Jesus whose name is "Prince of Peace." When you go to Him immediately to get it right, then you will *live* in peace. So let peace and comfort guide your heart."

"If you don't have peace about something, then before you do anything else, pray about what you're getting ready to do or what you are concerned about. Don't get in a hurry and try to do things on your own. The enemy will try to push you into his thinking and ways of doing things but Holy Spirit is loving and gentle. He gently nudges your conscience to go His way. Just talk in your encoded language from heaven that Holy Spirit gave you and He will guide you in the right direction."

"If you live your life that way, people will want to know how and why you are so happy and peaceful. The world is searching for peace in all the wrong places; drugs, alcohol, sex, new cars, bigger and better houses, higher education, business promotions, etc. but peace is only found in following the Prince of Peace and His Holy Spirit."

"Wow, you're so knowledgeable and those are all really good things to know." I told her. "I'm telling you, Zoë, you're really fortunate to have pastors for parents. They must teach you a lot or you just have a lot of wisdom or something. That must be one of the reasons why I enjoy spending time with you. I feel so peaceful when I'm with you. Now our friendship is going to be even more special because we have all this in common with each other. *I'm so excited!* So, are you *serious, we are really going to be sisters now?* We're going to have so much to talk about. I want you to teach me as much as you know, okay? I'm so interested in discovering all the things about God that I never knew before. I'm also very thankful that you told me the *truth* and that you brought me here this weekend. I will always have you to thank for introducing me to my Heavenly Father, to my Lord Jesus, and to my Teacher and Guide, Holy Spirit. I'm already so thrilled about my new life and it's only the first day!"

"One more thing for now," Zoë interjected, "you'll want to get started reading God's Word, the Bible. If you have ever tried reading it before and it didn't understand it, now it will start to make sense. The Word of God will become the most interesting book you read. You will realize that the more you learn, the more there is to learn. You won't be able to put it down and since you're already good at reading books anyway, you'll have no problem finding time to read the Bible. Holy Spirit will open up your understanding of what you are reading."

"Yeah, that's pretty close to what Stephanie said too," I agreed. "Thank you so much for all your great advice. *You are a true friend!* Oh, and do you know what else? You never told me what Elder Jeff said to *you* last night. *I'm so sorry* I've been so consumed with my own life, I didn't even bother to ask you what happened to you!"

"Oh, Selima," exclaimed Zoë, "I totally understand! This is *the* most important thing you will ever do in your entire life! It's a matter of forever being with God or separated from Him, *eternal life or death, heaven or hell!* What could possibly be more important than that? What Elder Jeff basically told me is that I have been given a gift to present the message of God's kingdom in a way that people can understand and except. He said that the Lord would use my gift mightily to bring many to believe in Jesus Christ. The best part is, since he spoke that word, I have already had the privilege of introducing you to Him, my very best friend in the world. *I am so excited too!* You know that it only gets better from here, right!"

"Wow, Elder Jeff sure knows how to hear clearly from God." I added. "I hope I will be able to do that someday, too."

"You never know. It sounds like God has great plans for you so I don't see why He wouldn't want you to know His voice that well." Zoë encouraged. "What time is it? Is it almost time for service?"

6

That Wasn't Me

"*Y*ah, *I think we had better get going!* It is getting close to time for the morning meeting to start. Right now its 10:10 and I want us to get a good seat towards the front. For some reason, I feel like I need to take my flute with me to the meeting."

"You'd better do it. That's probably Holy Spirit prompting you to follow His guidance. He always wants to bless us in some way or teach us something if we follow what He's leading us to do."

"*Do you think?* Could He be leading me and I actually heard Him talking to my spirit? *Oh, sweet!* I wonder why I would need to take my flute. I still don't know any of the music. I guess we'll just have to wait and see what happens.

"*I'm so thrilled inside I can't even describe my feelings! I'm sure nothing can top how I feel right now! I am so happy, I can barely contain myself!* Why do you suppose I would need to bring my flute?

I'm pretty sure I didn't learn the music while I was sleeping. *Or, at least I don't think I did!"* I giggled.

"Let's just see what happens." Zoë added eagerly. "I know the meeting is going to be so good this morning, especially after last night! Of course, you didn't get the full meaning of what Elder Jeff was saying last night. I'll tell you later what he taught about now that you'll be able to more understand. I could tell you were off somewhere else in your mind last night. But, you'll get so much more from the service this morning because the Holy Spirit will be teaching your heart the things that are being said. And maybe, He has a special song for you to play on the flute, you never know."

You know what, my special friend? I guess anything could be possible. I *did* pray in my encoded language for quite a while last night. I wonder what I was praying about. Maybe Holy Spirit was praying through me to learn music that I didn't know before. Would that be like opening up one of those "portals of power"? This is all just so amazing but also very mysterious!

As we went into the morning meeting, I had butterflies in my stomach wondering what was going to happen. I felt like something new and exciting was about to take place but I really couldn't image what. If it really *was* Holy Spirit encouraging me to bring my flute, then what would I be doing with it besides playing it? There was no reason that I could think at the moment. I'm quite sure He would know whether I knew the music or not, which I'm pretty sure I don't!

Zoë and I found a place to sit close to Becky and Mark. I was certain there was still a really big grin on my face, because when we sat down, Elder Jeff immediately rushed over to us and asked me why I was so happy? Zoë jumped up and announced to the whole room that I had given my heart and life to the Lord last night and that I was now a member of the family of God. Everyone began clapping and cheering and everyone started gathering around me and I was getting all kinds of welcomes and congrats and hugs and everything. It was kind of nice and fun but also quite embarrassing.

Elder Jeff then congratulated Zoë for her part in helping me to accept the Lord's free gift of salvation. He was excited that the word that she had received from the Lord the night before was already beginning to happen. Then he spotted my flute case under my seat. I think he must have remembered what the Lord had said through him last night about *me* because he got the biggest grin on his face! He leaned over and pointed to the case so I picked it up and handed it to him. He lifted it up in the air and showed everyone and then announced to everyone that the Lord had given me a message that I would play my flute for kings and important people and that people would get healed and freed of things when I played.

Okay, now I was getting really embarrassed! I think I must have turned three shades of red with embarrassment. There's nothing quite like spot-lighting a person, hello! So, was this why Holy Spirit wanted me to bring my flute, to confirm the Word that He had given to Elder Jeff last night? I wasn't sure but now there was more clapping and cheering and by this time I wanted to crawl under my chair.

Then, he came and leaned over, put his arm around my shoulder and gave me the most loving hug that I can ever remember receiving and every bit of embarrassment went out of me. All the love and joy and peace that I had felt earlier flooded my insides again. Tears rose to my eyes and began to spill out like big raindrops. This was another one of those memorable moments that I can hardly describe. It was like the closest thing to being hugged by God that I can imagine. Holy Spirit must have given that man a really *big* heart of love because it felt like it was just pouring out of him and into me. It was like every bit of hurt that I had ever experienced in my whole life had just melted away. How could one brief hug do all *that*? Wow, I'm so glad I came here this weekend. *This has already been so amazing!* What else could possibly take place?

The next thing I knew, I was down on the floor again floating and feeling light as a feather. *How does that happen?* This all was so new to me! Everyone around me acted like this was normal. Maybe all these things *were* normal after you have stepped through these "portals" into the supernatural realm. I sat up while I was still on the floor to get my bearings before getting back up into my seat. It was then that I noticed that the musicians had already gone up on stage and were getting ready to play their first song. Elder Jeff rushed over and knelt down beside me to ask if I would like to play my flute with them. I told him that I wasn't familiar with the songs that they were playing and singing.

That's when he made a surprising statement that at first made me a little hesitant but then gave me a boost of new courage and boldness. He said, "You might just like to try it anyway since Holy Spirit can anoint you and teach you to play what you might not have thought you knew at first. He can use your abilities and play through you. This may be an opportunity to open up one of those "hidden portals of power" God told you about last night!"

Wow! This could be the start of something extraordinary! It sounded kind of intriguing to have Holy Spirit play through me and here was a group of people that I could feel accepted and comfortable with and if I made mistakes, I wouldn't really feel embarrassed. That feeling had left me completely with that 'loving hug' I had just received a little bit ago.

I reached over and got my flute out, put it together, blew in it a couple of times to warm it up, and then headed for the stage. A younger guy rushed over to set me up with one of their microphones. Oh, wait now, I wasn't so sure about playing into a mike at this point. Everyone would *for sure* be able to hear my mistakes *then!* But all fear was gone and a new braveness and determination came over me like a suit of armor.

I put the flute up to my lips and began to blow. The next thing I knew, I was hearing this beautiful flute music coming through the speakers from my flute and my fingers seemed to be playing just the right notes. I didn't know what song I was playing because very simply, **that wasn't me**! Holy Spirit had taken over and the other musicians seemed to just follow along with what I was playing. Or was I following along with what they were playing, I couldn't be sure which. Okay, *this was way out there!* This wasn't just extraordinary but this was out there into the supernatural realm someplace where I could never have imagined being before!

The other musicians seemed to be in awe too, for they were looking around at each other with puzzled but smiling expressions on their faces. I sensed that this was definitely a song they had never played either. Holy Spirit was playing the whole group like an orchestrated composition. *Wow, this was just too much!* Wait until my orchestra conductor hears about this! On second thought, he probably wouldn't believe me if I told him. I felt tears begin to rise in my eyes with all the emotions that were flooding my heart. This was such an awesome and beautiful moment as we continued to play on. It was the most amazing time I had ever experienced playing my flute with any group!

There was nothing like it that I could compare it to. It was touching others too, I noticed, because there were several youth with tears streaming down their faces as the atmosphere touched some-thing deep inside them. It was like a soothing and healing breeze blowing by, kind of like that 'hug' I had received earlier. Was this what Elder Jeff meant when he said people would get healed of things and the songs would open people's hearts? How very incredible this was! I was just so thankful to be a part of this moment.

All of a sudden, there was like this bright, misty cloud that surrounded us! It looked sparkly like a crystal rainbow inside and the atmosphere became very electrifying! Oh my gosh, the sound inside was so heavenly and pure, I started to think I had somehow gone to heaven! It became very difficult to keep standing because I felt like just floating away.

A hush settled over the whole room as everyone became aware that this was a *very supernatural or extraordinary moment!* We had stumbled upon the very Presence of the Lord, I think, and it was so incredible and inviting that everyone wanted to be a part of it. Little by little, everyone crept slowly up to the front to get closer to the stage and the "Cloudy Presence". Some were kneeling while others were lying with their faces down to the floor and the only way to describe it was that it was so sacred and awesome that no one could say a word.

Oh, Holy Spirit! Is this what You had in mind when You urged me to bring my flute in here? I can't even begin to think what would have happened if I didn't hear You or didn't take Your guidance and had shrugged it off as being nothing – just my imagination. Not that I could even begin to take credit for any of this but You must have known ahead of time what You wanted to do in here and I got to be part of it!

"I feel so completely privileged to be having this very special moment in Your Presence, Dear Lord. I wish everyone in the world could feel what I'm feeling right now! Since I'm experiencing this intimate time with You, Lord, I wouldn't want to be anywhere else. This misty "Presence" is so purifying and loving and inviting. It makes me love You and want more and more of You. Please let me know Your Presence is with me all the time. Please keep leading me and showing me what to do."

7

An Absolute Miracle

Icontinued to play my flute for a while along with the other musicians until suddenly, an explosion of excitement broke out! *I'm so serious, friend!* Youth were screaming and yelling, crying and jumping up and down and running up and down the aisles. Believe me; the silence was definitely broken at that moment!

Elder Jeff came up to the stage and took a microphone off a stand and asked who wanted to share what was happening to them. The first one to shout out and run up on stage was a boy about 11-12 years old who earlier had been wearing some glasses that look like the thickness of coke bottles! They made his eyes look really big like they were bulging out, but at *that* moment he was holding them in his hand and he was yelling, *"I can see, I can see!"*

His eyes were normal size without his glasses on, of course, and tears were streaming down his face.

Those were the only words he could manage to speak because he was so overcome with emotion that no words could express his joy and amazement. This was an extraordinary miracle, looking at how strong the magnification was on his glasses! I heard later that without his glasses, he was considered legally blind. What a beautiful thing our Lord did for that boy. He probably was made fun of often for having such thick glasses, but not any longer. Our loving Heavenly Father had miraculously given him back his sight. Wait until his family and friends hear about this!

He started running all over and he kept repeating, "Thank you, Jesus; thank you, Jesus." Then, he rushed over to a friend that he must have come with. They took each other by the hands and facing each other, started jumping up and down, crying and laughing. I'm telling you, *it was such a special moment to experience with him!*

But that was only the first thing that happened. A girl that was sitting next to Melissa ran up to the front and started screaming at the top of her lungs, "Oh, my God, my *back* doesn't hurt, my back is healed! *Jesus healed my back!* I've had scoliosis, which is a curvature of the spine, since I was a little girl but *look*, I can bend over *and the pain is completely gone*! I couldn't do that before!"

She began to cry as she demonstrated that all her pain was gone by bending way over and touching the floor, and then she started running around everywhere in her excitement! She seemed so sure that her back had been straightened in that moment of time.

It was just so incredible to see what God was doing in that place.

Suddenly, a girl towards the back of the room who came running up to the stage and yelled, "*I can hear your flute with my right ear! Jesus, Jesus, Jesus! Oh, praise the Lord! I haven't been able to hear out of my right ear since I was three!* I had a really bad disease with a high fever and lost my hearing in this ear *but now I can hear perfectly! Oh my gosh, does anyone have a cell phone? I've got to call my mother!*"

"*Oh yes, me too! I've got to call my family and tell them all about this!*" the young boy chimed in.

An adult chaperone jumped up to hand them her cell phone and then, as she got closer to the front, she exclaimed that she was hearing angels sing. "It's the most beautiful choir sound I've ever heard. Can anyone else hear them? *Oh, it's so beautiful, it's so beautiful!*" she kept exclaiming, over and over, as big tears were dripping down her cheeks.

Then, right at that very instant I heard the whole stage fill with the sound of music as if a large orchestra was playing their instruments and a huge choir was singing so beautifully, I felt sure we were experiencing what it must be like to be in heaven. I was so stunned! I could no longer stand nor could I play my flute so I just knelt down until I was laying flat on the floor. Then, I began to shake uncontrollably. Behind me I could hear what must have been an angel and as I listened, it sounded like someone was taking a harp out of its case. Then I heard its strings beginning to be strummed so beautifully that

I could no longer focus on anything else, it was so magnificent!

I really wanted to actually turn around to see if it was an angel playing the harp but I couldn't move my head or my body. It was as if I was pinned to the floor! The more I tried to move my head and body, the more it felt like I was sinking deeper and deeper into the floor. It felt like the parts that were touching the floor weighed so much I couldn't budge them, like my body had turned into stone! I laid there just listening and enjoying the beautiful atmosphere since there wasn't anything *I could do!* Oh please, dear Holy Spirit, enjoying this moment in Your Presence is just so wonderful, I never want You to leave my side!

While I was enjoying the sound of the harp, it felt like someone was putting their hand on my head and immediately a flood of power rushed through my body like some kind of shock treatment or a really strong burst of energy raced through me. I couldn't see anyone by me and no one walked up to me so I don't know who could have done that. Do you think it was also an angel, friend? That's my guess since it wasn't like anything I've ever felt before. *Wow! This was all so extremely supernatural, I've never experienced anything so unbelievable in all my life!* I'm telling you, I'll *never* forget this as long as I live!

Wow! If this was what being a Christian was like, what had I been missing out on my whole life? My life had changed dramatically just since last night. I've never had so many new experiences in a twelve-hour period in all my life! Was this what it meant to open up "portals of power"? If I were to guess what that meant, I'd have to say that it's when you open up a portal or a passageway into the heavenly supernatural realm and God's wonders and miracles began to pour through. Gosh! They sure had been pouring through on *this* particular day!

I don't know if everyone had heard the angels like that chaperone and I were hearing them, but after a short time of being on the floor, Elder Jeff jumped up and ran back up to the front of the stage, grabbed a microphone again and started shouting, "It's all been a marvelous miracle, *an absolute miracle!* The Lord has visited us in the most spectacular way this morning and the angels have come into this place to join us in worshipping Him. We must give Him praise and thanksgiving and adoration! *Thank You, Jesus! Praise You, Lord! You are so awesome and amazing! Who could compare with You?"*

"*Do you realize what has just happened to Selima just now?"* he yelled out. "Our Lord has flowed through her instrument in a very special way today to minister to us, which confirms the prophetic word that He gave her last night. It's already beginning to happen. This has all been *completely supernatural!* What a privilege it is for us all to be a part of what our God is doing at this time. *Oh, give Him praise!"*

Everyone got *so extremely loud* at that moment. You would have thought you were in a sports stadium when the home team was winning. Everyone was screaming, cheering, clapping, laughing, crying, and jumping up and down! It was such an exciting moment; I can hardly express how spectacular it was. I was in so much awe of what the Lord did and was doing. I continued to lie on the floor of the stage because *I still couldn't move!* All I could do was soak in the entirely wonderful atmosphere that was in that place.

Out of the corner of my eye, I could see that Elder Jeff had also knelt down on the floor with his face towards the floor and was just weeping and praying and praising the Lord for the longest time. He was so overwhelmed with emotions, probably because of what had just happened and it brought tears back into *my* eyes.

He didn't move from that position for so long that others began to do the same thing, kneeling down or lying on the floor beside the stage. Soon it was absolutely quiet again with only an occasional sob. No one moved and no one spoke. The atmosphere returned back to the "holy hush" that we had experienced before the miracles. This whole meeting, from the wonderfully loving hug to the music and healings, to the angels and the misty cloud of God's Presence, *has been a complete miracle!* Who could begin to describe it in words that could be expressed? You just had to be there. *If only Jason was here!* I so wish he could have experienced all this with me!

As I lay on the floor with my insides continuing to "shiver" and my outside frame "glued" to the floor, I just couldn't believe that Holy Spirit had given me an opportunity to play in that way without music and without even knowing what I was playing. I really had nothing to do with it. All I had to do was just trust that the notes I was playing were the notes and tune Holy Spirit wanted me to play at that moment. I was just a mouthpiece for Holy Spirit to play *His* song and do *His* work.

What a special privilege! He used my flute to play for the youth in that place and then He began to do miraculous things that no person could have done. It was so very amazing but so humbling to have even a little part in that. You know, I'm no one special! I sure didn't deserve to be given that kind of a gift but then, I guess gifts are given, not earned. It was so special that I'll never forget it. *I'm telling you, I will never be the same again!* The idea that those kids had experienced such special miracles was so beyond belief. It was completely supernatural and incredible!

The place was quiet for about 15 – 20 minutes, maybe longer before Elder Jeff got up again and took the microphone. He stood there speechless for the longest time. Then he asked if anyone was present that didn't know the Lord of all these miracles. He told them to please raise their hands so that he could lead them in a prayer of commitment to the Lord. He prayed a prayer that they could all repeat and several raised their hands and prayed with him. He then said that there was nothing else that he could say or do that would be as important and life changing as what the Lord was already accomplishing. He dismissed the meeting and told everyone they could stay in the presence of the Lord and His holy angels as long as they wanted and that lunch would be served around 12:30.

It was somewhere around 11:30-11:45 at that time. Hardly anyone moved and no one spoke for what seemed like forever. It seemed like a *very* long time before I was able to move again since I was seemingly 'stuck' to the floor. I'm sure that this was another type of miracle since I had never heard of anyone "penned" to the floor, unable to move. I wonder if Zoë had ever heard of this before. Not that I wanted to move, not wanting to miss a second of this special environment. For a while longer, during the time when everyone else was still motionless, I continued to hear the angels worshipping the Lord.

I knew my life was forever changed and so deeply impacted that I would always want to spend time in His presence as much as I could. Nothing is greater than the feeling of being filled with the presence of the Lord. There is just nothing else that even compares with the feelings of peace and extreme love and acceptance I feel coming from His awesome presence.

The rest of that day is pretty much a blur in my memory for I must have just floated through everything after that. I know we went out to the lake and swam and sunned but I was so filled with His presence that everything else was so insignificant in comparison with what I experienced in that morning meeting and experiencing His presence filling my whole being for much of the day. My beautiful new life with my Lord had begun and I was enjoying the glow that I had felt from the moment I woke up.

We were served a very nice evening meal and then afterwards, everyone said their good-byes and gave their hugs. I knew I would see some of those youth again since these were all a part of my new family now. Zoë promised to get phone numbers and email addresses from some of the girls in our cabin and others we had met. I was just too "out of it" to do much of anything but just love on people and smile. I was so strongly affected by the intense presence of the Lord on me! It was incredible!

I remember riding home in the van with Zoë's family and saying that I had so much to tell Jason and my parents, but I must have needed help with the rest because I just got lost in the love of the Lord. I'm sure they understood because it had been such a life changing time for me!

They were respectful to give me my space and didn't ask me a lot of questions as to how I had enjoyed my time at the retreat. I know everyone in that car was deeply impacted by the morning meeting. I looked over at Zoë and she gave me the most loving smile that I knew she was filled with the Lord's presence too. She leaned over towards me and we embraced with a new love and appreciation for each other. We felt as close to each other as if we really were born as sisters. Holy Spirit had put a new bond of love in our hearts for each other that would last forever.

We arrived home early Saturday evening around 7:45 and the only thing I could think about was getting to my room and closing the door so I could spend the rest of the night with the Lord. I would catch my family up on the retreat later, but I was not ready to talk to anyone quite yet. I had a great deal of feelings and emotions and excitement that I needed to sort out first.

Over the course of the next week, I began to tell my family about all the incredibly wonderful and miraculous things that had happened at the retreat. At first, they didn't believe the things I was telling them but as I began to change and talk differently and want to spend more time alone in my room so I could be with my Lord, they began to realize that I was for real.

The week after the retreat, Zoë came over to visit and began to share with Jason some of the things she had taught me and because he was beginning to get familiar with the "new" me, he wanted to receive Jesus as his Lord also. That was *the most beautiful moment!* He had tears in his eyes and his heart was so tender and loving toward the Lord and to us as well. Zoë was so incredibly knowledgeable and informative that who wouldn't want to choose to follow their Lord? She truly did have a gift for presenting the information.

It didn't take long for Mom and Dad to see that this is what they wanted to do also. We asked Zoë to come over one evening and we all sat around the kitchen table and she taught and then we all prayed together. I feel so fortunate to have had a small part in bringing my own family into the family of God and Zoë was skilled in using her gift. Can you imagine what has changed in our lives as a result of this? We have become such a close knit and loving family. Jason and I have had so much more to share with each other and we have become much more aware of the ways of the Lord since then.

Zoë's parents became our pastors and we have gotten much closer with their family as well and it has been so exciting to discover all of the aspects to our destiny in the Lord. Over the course of the next few months after that weekend, several of our extended family members became followers of Jesus Christ as their Lord as well and it has been so rewarding to see our earthly family members become our eternal family as well.

Jason and I went out and bought several CD's & MP3's of the new music that I had discovered at the retreat that we have downloaded onto our computers and our ipods. We spend such intimate times just listening to the music and learning the Bible together. When either of us learns something new that the Lord is teaching us, we always share it with each other. We have gained such a bond in the Lord that we would have never experienced otherwise and it's so indescribable how close we have become. We've become very close to Zoë as well, our "holy threesome" as we have started to call ourselves.

8

Returning to the Present

My thoughts are now *returning* back *to the present*, on this November afternoon, laying here on my bed. Thinking back on that spring two and a half years ago, my insides have been completely flooded with all the emotions and feelings of that miraculous weekend that changed me and my family's destiny forever. The shaking I experienced all night last night until a little while ago was the same sensation I had felt back then while I was laying on the stage that morning after I had been playing my flute for the Lord. Now I know that all that has happened to me has been for a reason and a purpose, and it has prepared me for what just went on last night and what is yet to take place in my future. There is a definite connection between them all.

I can't wait to tell you and Jason about last night. He always seems to be gone when the really exciting things happen. Maybe the next time something fantastic happens, he will be the one that experiences it. This afternoon is just passing so slowly waiting for him to get back home. Hopefully, he'll be back this afternoon and not later on this evening! I just wished that I had gotten Micah's cell phone number so I could call him and tell him I'm desperate to talk to Jason!

I think I will pray for a while in my heavenly language. I haven't spent much time playing video games or watching TV lately, so the most useful thing I could do with my time right now is to speak in my encoded heavenly language. Besides, there's not much to watch on a Saturday afternoon anyway. If there's time after that, I'll probably read some more in my new book that I just got entitled <u>End of the Spear.</u> That is, if Jay doesn't return by then. I've just started it and it is quite interesting! It's based on a true story and it's the kind of adventure that you'd think could only be made up!

You know, my friend, you can choose to pray in your supernatural language any time you want to talk to Father God or our Lord Jesus. Holy Spirit is always with us, ready to pray through us whenever we want. In fact, I believe that He anxiously waits for the moment when we allow Him the privilege to pray through us to our Lord and Father because those are some of our most perfect and effective prayers. I always feel His presence with me when I start praying in His encoded language. It's a way of entering His presence *on purpose!* And, I'm convinced that spending time in His presence is *the greatest, most powerful and beneficial thing a person can do in this life!*

Besides being in His presence, another advantage to praying in our heavenly language is being a partner with God in what He is doing in this world. It is such an awesome privilege to know that our prayers could be for someone clear across the planet that has no one else to pray for them! We won't know about everything our prayers accomplished for other people until we go to be with our Lord at the end of this age.

The Bible says that it also builds up our faith if we pray in our Holy Spirit language. I want my faith built up to believe for the awesome things that the Lord has planned for my life. I could be praying for myself to be ready for when I meet up with some king somewhere or someone like that. I like that the Lord has all kinds of mysteries for us to search out. It's like a treasure hunt. You know, the Bible is like that. It is just like a treasure chest of surprises waiting to be found out.

If you have asked Jesus to be your Lord as a result of what I experienced on my "weekend of destiny", and you haven't yet begun to speak in your encoded language, just ask Jesus to fill you with His Holy Spirit and give you His gift. He is so willing to give it to you because He wants to have that communication with you and through you.

Remember though, that *you* have to do the *speaking* and He will do all the rest. Just don't try to *think* about it too hard because sometimes your mind gets in the way of your spirit doing the talking. If you turn off your brain and just let Holy Spirit do the talking, it's quite simple. The difficulty comes when we try to think of words to say and then the flow of words doesn't come.

You will sense that the words are coming up from your belly rather than from your head. Just start speaking those words out and they may sound funny at first but pretty soon a whole new language will be flowing out of your mouth that you didn't even learn. Just think, you can do something supernatural every day and pretty soon it won't seem supernatural at all. It will just become natural.

It's just like that *falling down* stuff. At first, it was really pretty strange to me, but now that I have been around it for the past couple of years, it's seems almost natural. It's called "falling out under the power" or being "slain in the Spirit". Whatever you want to call it, it is just when Holy Spirit's power comes on you so heavily that your physical body can't contain it and it just goes limp.

So anyway, I'm going to speak in my encoded language for a little while now, before Jason gets home. I want to tell you about last night at the same time I'm telling him so while I'm praying in my heavenly language, why don't you speak in your language now, too?. "Holy Spirit, I pray that you will fill my friend with Your Holy Presence and give him or her, their own heavenly encoded language that You have provided for and want for them to receive. Thank you, Jesus. Amen."

After you have been speaking in your encoded language for a while, sometimes Holy Spirit will tell you what you have been praying or speaking about. It's called the "interpretation of tongues". It's not called a translation because that would be word for word, although sometimes that happens too. Mostly you'll just be able to get the understanding of what it is you are praying or speaking about.

Sometimes Holy Spirit will tell you what someone else is saying in his or her encoded language. After you've been speaking in your language for a while, sometimes you will receive other languages that sound totally different from the first one you receive, which is all really amazing. This whole subject of tongues or encoded languages is all very supernatural. But then, our God is a supernatural God and He wants His children to experience His supernatural gifts. It pleases Him greatly when we step out in faith and believe Him to help us do all kinds of supernatural things! *I'm convinced that this is the most exciting life there is!*

That's why I so desperately want to tell you about last night. It was so extraordinary and exciting! I hope I can adequately put it into words so you two can know what it was like. If only Jason would hurry home! I've got to tell him soon because I am about to burst with emotions over all the things God did through me (and others) that are so intimate. These kinds of things you just don't want to share with anybody! Sometimes I feel that if I shared my most personal thoughts with just any person, they would laugh or make fun or blow it off as not being all that special and *that's just plain embarrassing!* When you share it with someone close who knows you, they know how to keep it more special and confidential. Do you know what I mean?

Do you have someone you can share your most secret thoughts and feelings with? I hope so. It's really special to have a close friend like that. I have two, Jason and Zoë, actually three, including Holy Spirit. I can talk to Him at any time anywhere because He is always with me, and He's always with you too, if you have made Jesus your Lord. If you haven't, I hope you will want to do that very soon. He can be your very special confidante as well.

Oh, I think I hear a car running outside! That could be Jason getting back home from Micah's! I'm hearing a car door shut and now the back door has just slammed shut. *"Jason, is that you?"* I called out.

"Yah, it's me." he answered back, "What's up, Lima?" (That's his pet name for me – "LEE'-mah")

"I've been waiting for you forever, it seems! Please come up to my room. I have got *so much to share with you!*"

"You do? Just a minute, I need to get a drink of milk first. I'll be *right up,*" he hollered back.

"Hurry, would you? I've been waiting *all day to talk to you!* You won't *believe* what happened last night!"

"Okay, okay! I'm coming, I'm *coming! Gosh, I just get in the door and you're already hounding me up a storm!"* he teased. "Give me a minute to get settled. Let me put my bag up in my room and I'll be right there, okay?

"There you are, finally!" I exclaimed as he came through my bedroom door. "Oh, Jason, I have been waiting to talk to you since last night and ever since I woke up this morning! I need to put Micah's phone number in my cell in case I need to talk to you urgently again. *You weren't answering your cell and it's been really agonizing waiting for you all this time and not getting a chance to tell you what has happened!"*

"Okay, I'll get it for you" Jason replied, "and sorry, I forgot to charge my battery but what is *so important? What* are you *so desperate to tell me? What* happened last night that's got you *so fired up that you can't give me even a single moment of peace?"*

"Oh, Jason, stop!" I responded to his teasing, "*It's not that bad!"*

9

Night of Wonders

"Really, Jason, I wish you had come with me last night. You missed out on one of *the* most awesome **night of wonders** that I've ever experienced in my entire life! There were so many supernatural things happening and *I have been shaking all night long!"*

"It's only been in the last hour or so that my body has finally stopped vibrating. I'm sure the vibration of my body was because so much of God's power was flowing through me! It reminds me of when I had that happen to me at the retreat. Do you remember me telling you about that?" Jason nodded.

"Anyway," I continued, "Zoë's folks found out that this special prophet was passing through town and arranged to have him come to our church for a special meeting at the last minute. I helped call around to let some people know about it. I knew you had already planned to go to Micah's so it didn't even cross my mind to tell you to come with me to this meeting instead. Of course, I had no idea what would happen, but I *promise* I will *definitely* let you know about anything else that happens like this in the future."

"What? Wait a minute, Selima!" Jason interjected furiously. *"Let me get this straight! You mean to tell me that you called all these people to tell them about this prophet coming to our church and you didn't even bother to tell me? How did you know that I wouldn't have chosen to go there instead of Micah's, or even have invited him to go with me?"*

"I know now that I should have told you regardless. I'm so sorry I wasn't thinking. I hope you will forgive me! Just to let you know though, the prophet is going to be at our church tomorrow for the morning and night meetings. So, maybe the Lord will do even more amazing things through him in the meetings tomorrow, who knows?"

"Anyway, the prophet's name is Bryan Hayes and Zoë's parents told us that he has traveled to lots of different countries, including the Holy Land. He recently went to Africa to speak to a crowd and they estimated there were somewhere *between 8-10 million people that attended one single service! Can you imagine that? I can't even begin to picture that!"*

"He's supposed to have some video footage of one of those meetings and *the people stretch on and on for about two whole miles! It's almost too mind boggling to even fathom!* He might show us the video tomorrow during one of the services, but I don't know for sure. I hope he does, anyway. He's not very well known in our country yet, but he's *tried* to stay more anonymous and not promote himself too much on television or radio shows."

"Zoë's parents came by to pick me up on their way to church and when we got there last night, it was shortly before 6:00. The meeting was scheduled to start at 7:00 but many people started coming between 6:00 and 6:15 to join us in prayer. By 6:30, the room was loud with the sound of people praying, mostly in their supernatural language. We were all praying for the meeting; the prophet, the music team and for the people who would be coming."

"Lots of people were there that I had never seen before so I suspect that some of the ones we called must have invited others that *they* knew. People were starting to stand against the sides and back wall of the church and out into the foyer. By the time 7:00 rolled around, there was not an empty seat in the house. The place was *packed* with people!"

"You know, Jay, there was such an atmosphere of high expectation and anticipation that you could actually feel it tangibly thick in the air. It was really exciting that all those people had chosen to come to *our* church. I'm guessing it wasn't so much *our church* they were coming for, though. Obviously they came to see and hear the great things that have been happening with this prophet and see what the Lord might do through him again. The Lord has certainly used him quite a bit to demonstrate His miraculous awesome power!"

"Pastor John and Debra, were sitting in their usual spot on the front row. Just moments before 7:00, one of the ushers escorted Prophet Bryan up to his seat next to them. A hush came over the room as soon as he entered and all eyes were on him as he walked down the aisle to his seat."

"He's a fairly tall, thin built man who's probably in his late 40's with a mustache and goatee. His dark hair is wavy and starting to gray a bit and he wears it a little longer in the back but really nicely styled."

"Oh, so what you're really saying is that you think he's handsome." Jason teased.

"Now stop, I didn't say that, but I guess I'm not denying it either. But come on, he's certainly too old for me. But he is "easy on the eyes" as they say. He has a nice deep, kind voice with a slight accent and he's got quite the captivating smile and manner about him. I'd say he's from the Mediterranean somewhere but that's only a guess."

"A little bit after 7:00, after briefly talking to the prophet, Pastor John walked up to one of the microphones on the platform and introduced our guest and then asked the music team to please take their places. I grabbed my flute and bottled water and hurried to my mike."

(Oh, by the way, my friend, I didn't tell you that after I came back from that retreat two years ago, Pastor John asked me to start learning to play the songs they sang and join their music team. Sometimes, I sing on the music team with the other singers but most of the time I just play my flute. Since I have my own mike for my flute, I can sing whenever I'm not playing but last night I was up there mostly to play my flute.)

"We started the song service with upbeat songs and when we moved into the slower and more worshipful songs, I started playing my flute more. A couple of times, I soloed on the flute while the drummers and the keyboarder accompanied me. Our banner twirlers were waving and swinging their flags beautifully and powerfully on both sides of the stage."

"So, get this, Jay! While I was playing a solo towards the end of our song list, Prophet Bryan *jumps up out of his seat, hops up onto the platform and races over to me and says, "Keep playing; just keep playing! That's beautiful!* The angels are gathering in this room to hear the saints worshipping their God and *they've come to join with us in worship!"*

"They seem to be enjoying your flute playing," he continued, "so don't stop playing that song. The angels are bringing the atmosphere of heaven into this place and we are beginning to experience heaven on earth. Get ready for what is about to happen next, because the supernatural is about to break out!"

"Thank you for that flute music, Miss. It sounds like a song straight from *heaven!* What is your name, daughter?" he turned and asked me."

"Selima Jeruelli," I replied back to him."

"Then he smiled really big and said this to me, Jay, "Selima, *Ah*, Selima, what a *beautiful* name. I have traveled all over the world and I've spent a great deal of time in the Holy Land and you have a very significant name! *'Jeruel'* means 'founded upon, established and made firm in the things of God' and *'Selima'* is the old Chaldean word for 'Shalom, Salem or Solomon' meaning 'peace and prosperity'. Together they make up the name of the Holy City 'Jerusalem'."

"I pray for such peace and prosperity to be upon you, my child." he declared, laying his palm on my forehead, *"and you shall truly be made firm and founded upon the Word and His principles and firmly established in the ways of the Lord. You shall play your flute for kings and priests of many nations of the world where our Father shall take you! The songs of the Lord will bring peace, prosperity and the favor of God upon those you shall play for. Get ready for an even greater pouring out of His Spirit upon your life for you shall see many miracles, signs and wonders! You are chosen of God to do great exploits for His namesake!"*

"Oh, Jay, do you know what? That was really similar to what Elder Jeff spoke over me at the retreat. *Can you believe it? This is such an exciting life!* I can't even imagine playing my flute for a king or a president, anybody like that. I know I don't play *that well* so it *has* to be Holy Spirit doing all the playing through me, like He does sometimes, for all that to happen, ya know?"

"Having a part in other people's miracles is what is so special for me. It's just too awesome to think that He chose my flute playing for such a special purpose. I just can't even imagine why He chose **ME**! Who am I? I'm certainly not anyone special and no different from you, Jason. But our God is so supernatural that it's just His nature to want to do for us what we can't do for ourselves. I'm sure He has a very special plan for you, too. We can be a brother-sister team or a threesome with Zoë."

"I'm just so grateful that He called our family into *His* heavenly family. We'll never be able to repay the Lord for all that He has done for us. But it feels right to want to do *something to give back whatever we can in His service, don't ya think?* It's pretty cool that our last name is from the Holy Land. I wonder if Mom and Dad knew when they named me Selima that the two names together make up the name "Jerusalem". It's kind of special to be connected to the Holy Land with our name, don't you agree, Jay? Do you know what your name means?"

"Yeah, it *is* pretty cool." Jason answered. "Oh, no I don't remember what the name "Jason" means. But I think there's someone in the Bible named Jason, though. Do you think Dad's family knows that our last name Jeruelli is from the name Jeruel - part of the name Jerusalem? We should look into this more. Maybe we have some kind of Jewish background somewhere or something. That would be pretty interesting, all right. So, what else happened? I can hardly believe that the only thing that you have been all worked up over was just about your name and that he confirmed the word from the retreat. Not that what he said to you isn't important. It's really cool. God must have some very big plans for you. But, is there more that you haven't told me about yet?"

"Yes, yes, don't get so impatient! I like to take it slow and savor all the details. That's how God wired girl's brains, ya know. And mine is no exception!

And guys just like to get all the facts, right? That's how he made you. But just let me "*live the moment*" a little bit. After all, that's why I like talking to you about things. You understand me so well and we can express ourselves without being embarrassed or self-conscious. Thank you for being my close friend and confidante. It means a lot to me."

"I appreciate you being my friend and confidante, too", Jason added. "We've certainly gotten a lot closer through our times with the Lord, huh?" With that statement, we gave each other a warm hug.

10

Projecting Power

"There's so much more to tell you still. Are you ready for what I'm about to tell you next, Jay?" I asked him with a teasing smile on my face.

"Just hurry and tell me, would you?" Jay insisted as he smirked back. "You have been keeping me in *so much suspense ever since I walked in the door! What amazing thing happened that you're taking so long to tell me?"*

"Well, immediately after Prophet Bryan spoke that prophetic word over me about my name, with his palm touching my forehead, I fell to the floor like a limp noodle. The powerful Presence of the Lord coming through the prophet's hand poured over my body and I instantly lost my ability to keep standing. But, that's when it starts getting really good, Jay. Right at that moment, I became aware of something large to my left and realized that a huge angel was standing there beside me. It was very scary and so awesome and holy all at once. I started to shake just at the thought of him being there, but then, an unbelievably soothing feeling swept over me that instantly stopped my body from trembling."

"You know, *I could actually feel some kind of emanating **power projecting** off of him and pouring into my body like he was giving me an injection of the supernatural power of the Lord!* Do you think that this was another "portal of power" I had passed through to have this experience, Jay? *I am sure of it!* Anyway, so while I was lying there, I suddenly realized that I was still holding onto my flute. *Oh, Jason, you couldn't, **in a million years**, guess what happened next! Get this! That huge angel very gently picked me up off the floor and set me back up on my feet right in front of my mike and made a gesture like he wanted me to play some more!*"

"*What? No way!*" Jason burst out. "*You mean to tell me that an angel actually picked you up and put you back on your feet again? Oh, I can hardly believe that!*"

"I swear to you that I'm telling you the truth, Jason. How could I lie at a time like this? I'm not sure but it's possible that Prophet Bryan might have seen him do that, too. I don't think anyone else saw it, though, or even knew that there was an angel beside me at all. It was right after the angel stood me back up that Prophet Bryan continued to say to me while he was still being miked, "Yes, my daughter, continue to play your flute for you are bringing us right into the Throne Room of God."

"You know, Jay, I didn't think about this until just now while I'm telling you about it, but possibly the prophet could have motioned for the angel to pick me up, like he knew all along that he was there. Jason, it was like he was waiting for me to stand back up so that he could tell me to keep playing. *I am definitely asking him about this one!*"

"Next, he said to me, still on the mike, "The angels have come to join you in the "Song of the Lord". For those of you who can hear the sound of heaven, listen very closely with your spirit ears for this is a *very rare* occasion. Let's lift up our hands and worship the King of Kings and Lord of Lords with the angels. He is worthy to be worshipped!"

"So when I began to play my flute again, I felt this surge of strength fill my body and this beautifully fresh air filled my lungs. As the notes began to flow out, it was *so incredible!* He must have given me some kind of *heavenly air* because I felt completely empowered to play like never before. The notes came out effortlessly light and airy and the tune that Holy Spirit directed me to play made the most beautiful sound that I can't even describe it."

"Hopefully, when we get the recording of the service, you'll be able to hear the difference in the sound. I can't even begin to take credit for the song or the sound for it was certainly not my own *at all*. Oh, Jason, it was *so awesome*, just telling you about it makes me feel all warm inside. Just wait until you hear the rest."

"I continued playing my flute while the keyboarder and drummers accompanied me and the more I played, the more energy flowed through my body and that huge angel continued to stand right beside me. *Then I heard it!* It was *the most beautiful sound* that earth has ever heard, seriously! The angels were singing and playing instruments just like at the retreat when I heard them before. *Oh, Jason! It was so incredible, who could begin to describe it?* You *must* hear it for yourself sometime very soon for *there is nothing on earth I can compare it with!* And the song I was playing on my flute was right in step with what they were playing. *Can you believe it, Jason, can you? I was actually playing with the angels and got touched by an angel!"*

"The next thing that happened was when Prophet Bryan began to shout that *miracles* were beginning to happen all over the room. (*Not like there weren't already some miracles happening!*) He exclaimed that two people received their eyesight back and that someone else got back their hearing! After that, he announced that several people were being healed of cancer and other kinds of diseases. Then, he shouted that whoever was in need of a miracle needed to come to the front quickly because God was pouring out His healing power!"

"People jumped up and ran up to the front of the church so fast that immediately there was no room left. People were pressing to get as close to the stage as possible and after the front was too full, they filled up the aisles and the sides, hoping to get a healing touch from the Lord. The prophet then looked over at me, gave me a beckoning wave with his hand, and said, "Selima, would you please come over here and play your flute over the people who have come forward? God is about to use your gift to flood His people with His presence!"

"I walked up front to center stage and began playing my flute over the crowd of people that were pressed to the front for their miracles from the Lord. The angel had moved with me and continued to stand next to me and then you could *never* imagine what happened *next!* There were several screams that rang out as, all of a sudden; the people began to fall back on each other like *dominos* right in front of me! I gasped in amazement and stopped playing my flute, totally in shock as I watched what was happening. Prophet Bryan immediately yelled, *"Keep playing, Holy Spirit is not finished yet!"*

"I put my flute back up to my lips to play and after just a few notes had immerged from my flute, the people down the aisles and down the sides started falling backwards and then the people in the two front rows fell over. After that, rows and rows of people began to fall over in their seats as the Presence of the Lord came pressing down upon the crowd like a heavy blanket which made it very difficult for everyone to continue to stand or sit up. It was such an unbelievable sight. *Oh, Jason, was this yet another portal to supernatural power? I had not spoken a word or touched anyone physically! All I was doing was playing my flute!"*

"There was not a word spoken by anyone as everyone looked like they had fallen into a "stupor", if you could call it that. No one moved even though many were lying on top of one another. The musicians who were originally accompanying me had fallen also but I couldn't tell that at first because there was still music accompanying me as I played. It was undoubtedly the angels who had completely taken over playing the music. If we have that recorded, you will be able to hear them playing with me. I sure hope that it's on there. That will be so incredibly awesome!"

"I know it had to be only to the angel's credit, standing beside me, that *I was still able to keep standing and playing!* I could tell he was continuing to infuse me with supernatural strength. Otherwise, I would have been like all the rest, laying down in a "stupor". The prophet knelt down and didn't speak for quite some time."

"Then, as I began to realize that I was the only one left still standing, I was overcome with emotions and began to sob. The Lord had again used my flute in a *supernatural* way and the "portals of power" being opened were becoming much more apparent. The Lord was really fulfilling what He had spoken at the retreat. It was happening all over again."

"I knelt down to worship the Lord for what He had done and was doing as tears came flowing out of my eyes and down my cheeks in a continual stream. I quickly ran out of words and began to pray in my heavenly language but could only get out a few sounds before I was overcome by the Presence and went out under the power like everyone else had. I don't know how long everyone was overcome by the power and presence of the Lord but when I came out of my "stupor", I heard gasps and screams coming from all parts of the room and some laughter and crying and all kinds of emotions as many people began expressing the miracles they were experiencing. There were so many that I can't begin to tell you, just that there were many miraculous healings and creative miracles."

"When I tried to stand up, I realized that I was shaking all over. That's when the shaking started and *didn't stop until this afternoon!* The angel that had been at my side had apparently left me then and I'm pretty sure that my physical body had now begun to react to all the power of the Lord that had surged through it, which was more than it has ever experienced or could possibly handle."

"When Prophet Bryan *did* get up to speak, he announced that whoever had a miracle happen in his or her body, needed to begin writing a testimonial about it. He encouraged everyone to get documents from doctors if they could. Then he said that he was going to get in touch with the local Cable TV News station and report the goodness of the Lord to the world. Wow! Can you *believe* it, Jason? Our church is going to be on the *news* sometime soon! But that wasn't all. Do you know what he did next? He walked over to me and asked the most awesome thing. He asked that if it was at all possible for me, that he would love it if I could do some traveling with him and play at his meetings!"

"Can you fathom it? It's too incredible to believe! I guess that's so that God gets all the credit for making it happen. Prophet Bryan said he would talk to Mom and Dad about me playing the flute for his meetings to see if anything could be arranged. I am so excited I can hardly contain myself! *Now, do you know why I couldn't wait to talk to you?* It's all so unbelievable I needed *someone* to confide in and not everyone would have listened without passing it off as some fairytale or something. You do believe me, right?"

"I have to admit that some of it is a little hard to believe but I know you wouldn't kid around about something so intimate with the Lord. What do you think Mom and Dad are going to say about you going with Prophet Bryan? Have you talked to them about it yet?" Jason inquired. "Were *they* even there last night?"

"Yes, they *did* come last night. They came after Zoë and I got there and they were just barely able to get a seat before it filled up. They drove me home but everyone was in so much shock and awe from the events that no one talked on the way back. I have been in my room most of the day just mulling everything over in my mind and since I was shaking for so long, I've mostly been just lying on my bed and daydreaming about it."

"The Presence of the Lord has still been so strong on me and you should have heard me laughing earlier. It was so loud and not anything like my laugh. I'm going to ask Zoë about it. I'm pretty sure it is something supernatural that happens when you are so full of God's presence. I'm surprised that Mom and Dad didn't come up here to see what was so funny. I'm guessing that they are also quite affected by last night's events because you just can't be in that kind of environment for long without being *changed for life!"*

"Do you think it will be anything like that tomorrow? I *really* feel like I missed out big time." Jason said quietly and sadly.

"I don't know, Jay. I wish I had told you about it instead of assuming that you'd still choose to go to Micah's. Yah, the only sad thing about last night is that *you* weren't there to *share* it with us. If I *do* get to travel with Prophet Bryan, I'm sure going to push for you coming with me. From now on, though, we have *got* to be prepared and anticipate that our Heavenly Father wants to do miraculous supernatural things in our lives *all the time with both of us!"*

"Well, with that said, we should *seriously* expect the supernatural to happen in tomorrow morning's service too, then." Jason added. "Well Lima, are you going to go talk to Mom and Dad about Prophet Bryan or not?"

"I don't know. Maybe I should just wait until tomorrow to let Prophet Bryan do all the talking since I might mess everything up if I say something wrong. If it comes from him, maybe it will have more validity."

"Yah, you're probably right," replied Jason. "If you open your mouth and say the wrong thing, you won't want to forgive yourself any time soon."

11

Bejeweled

"Jason, your hair is not the most important thing this morning! Please hurry up!" I yelled at him teasingly, "We have *got* to get to church early today. It's going to be so packed, I just know it. God is going to do some amazing things there today and I don't want to *miss a thing!*"

"I know, I know, I'm coming!" Jason yelled back. "Today is my day, today is my day," he added in a singsong voice.

"You know, I think you're right." I agreed as we climbed into the SUV to leave. "I just *know* that Father God has something very special planned for you today and I'm *am definitely* expecting supernatural things to happen and more portals to be opened. *I just can't wait!* I think it pleases the Lord when we believe that His Presence and supernatural power *is going to be displayed*, don't you?"

105

"I'm very sure you're right, Selima." Jake, their father broke in. "I believe He *does* enjoy that. In fact, His Word in Hebrews tells us that, 'It's impossible to please God *without faith* and that He's a Rewarder of those that really search for Him', and I know that you two have really been on an intense quest to really know Him and believe Him to do great things in your lives. I just believe He wants to reward *both of you today* for your anticipation of His miraculous signs and wonders. I think we *all* have a great expectation after what happened *Friday night!* Wasn't that so *remarkable?* I'm really sorry you weren't there, Jason."

"Yah, me too, don't remind me," Jason replied sadly and quietly. "That's why *today* is my day!" he added more energetically.

"Maybe Prophet Bryan will have a special word from the Lord for you today, Jason," Rachel, their mother, chimed in. "Let's just lift up this morning's service to the Lord. Father, we praise You this morning and ask You to visit us in a very special way today and bless the gifts You have given Prophet Bryan to demonstrate Your awesome power and glory. And Lord, if it be Your will, please meet and exceed Jason's expectations in a unique way today to assure him how much You love him and want to use him. Please show him the powerful destiny You have planned for him in Your kingdom, in Jesus Name, Amen."

"Amen!" Jake agreed with his wife's prayer. "Well, that was perfect timing, we're here. Selima, don't forget your flute. Let's hurry in there now and get a good seat. I'm sure it's going to fill up very fast after what happened Friday Night."

"Okay, Dad, I'll run in there right now and save us all a seat!" Jason called as he raced off towards the church doors. I could tell he was so excited about the service that he didn't want to take any chances of missing out on anything. We were sure glad he had hurried ahead of us to grab some seats, though. By the time we all got in there and got seated, within just a few moments, there was standing room only. I looked for Zoë and spotted her sitting with her parents and sister and brother on the front row. That means she'll probably be sitting near Prophet Bryan during the singing. I'm kind of glad I will be up on the platform playing my flute so I can see everything going on. Maybe I'll go sit next to her when we finish the singing if there is room when Prophet Bryan gets up to preach. Jason usually sits over on the left side of the sanctuary by all the other youth but today, because he saved us a seat, he ended up just staying next to us.

I could just feel the anticipation in the air like I had felt it on Friday night. What was going to happen today, I wondered? It was just so exciting to see everything the Lord had done on Friday in this place. So, could it get any better than that? My heart felt like it was racing and beating loudly, although I was the only one hearing it, I'm quite sure. This was like one of those prearranged appointments that God had set up for all the people that He chose to be in this room today and they were about to be shown His awesome power and goodness! I just knew He was about to do something spectacular and I was so very glad to be here at this moment! And also glad that *Jason* was here this time, too.

People were packing into every available spot including out in the foyer and down the hall to the restrooms. Every folding chair that could be found was being set up. There were people still standing and more were coming in. Word must have spread fast about what had happened on Friday.

"Oh, Dear Father in Heaven, please make this be a day that no one in this place will ever forget and change us forever! Give us faith to see the impossible and the extraordinary but keep our hearts pure before You so that we don't get prideful in any way. I love You and praise You ahead of time for what You are about to do. Thank you Father, in Jesus' Name, Amen."

"Let's stand up and praise the Lord," Pastor John announced as it turned 10:00 sharp. "This is a very special day today. We have Prophet Bryan Hayes with us this morning and if you weren't here Friday, you missed a *very* exciting time in the Presence of the Lord. Our Lord showed His greatness and love for us with many miraculous signs and wonders in this house of worship. In fact, Prophet Bryan wants to air some of your miracles on the local TV news station so that the world will know how *great* our God is. If you received a miracle on Friday, get in touch with our staff. We are compiling the testimonies as soon as we can. Get ready for the supernatural. Take it away, music team."

The first few songs were very lively with lots of clapping and dancing and even a few shouts from time to time. The people in the room were happy to be praising the Lord for His goodness and favor that He was showering upon His people. This was such an exciting moment in time as the expectation of His miracles was rising. Then, as we started playing a song with a more Jewish feel, both men and women began filling up the area between the front pews and the stage platform with lively dancing, which was quite liberating. Now this is what I call praising the Lord! There were so many shouts of joy and celebration to the Lord for His greatness and for all the things He had done and was about to do.

All of a sudden, Prophet Bryan jumped up on the stage and took a mike and began yelling, "*Get ready, get ready, get ready!* The Lord is in this house and He is about to show His Presence in a *mighty* way!"

I looked around to see where Jason was. He was up in the front of the pews next to the stage dancing and praising the Lord with the crowd that had gathered there. I had never seen him so free. He was only a few feet away from Prophet Bryan and he had the biggest smile on his face! I just knew that the Lord was about to answer his heart's cry.

Oh, my goodness! You can't even imagine what happened next, my friend! Right in the front, where all the people were praising Him so liberally, the most amazing thing began to happen! This sparkly metallic material began raining down upon the people out of mid-air and everyone that was in that area began to be covered with this stuff. In a matter of moments, many people began running to the front to get under this "sparkly rain". It was one of the most supernatural things that I have ever seen with my own eyes next to seeing the angel the other night!

Prophet Bryan yelled, "This is a miraculous manifestation of the Lord's glory!" He continued, "It's being called "glory dust" or "glory rain" for those of you who have never experienced it before." Then he added, "Along with this display of His Presence, He also changes people's fillings in their teeth to either gold, or platinum. Sometimes He even fills teeth that need fillings or fixing in some way. Believe for your teeth miracles! He cares for you and doesn't want you to have mercury in your amalgam fillings, which the medical profession is now finding to be not that good for your health, but God's ways are always higher than man's ways."

"Where is my flute player?" he asked. "Selima, could you please come over here to the front. Please play your flute over the people because God is not finished yet. He is just getting started, in fact. He has just announced His Presence but this is only the beginning."

Oh, my friend, it's hard to describe how very exciting this service is getting and it's only just barely begun. I rushed forward to the edge of the stage with my flute and began to play over the people who had already been showered with "glory dust". I looked over at Jason and he was literally covered. I was so happy for him!

As I played, the keyboarder and the drummer accompanied me and the Lord began to shower the "glory rain" all over me. It covered my flute and my clothes but I couldn't pay much attention to that just then, for the most beautiful flute music was flowing out of my flute effortlessly and it sounded like angels singing. Again, I couldn't even begin to take credit for this song for this was the Lord's song being played over His people and I just got to be the mouth and the fingers that He used to play His song.

All of a sudden, I felt a strange tightness in my teeth that had fillings, like I had just been to the dentist and had gotten new fillings. Do you know how sometimes when you have to bite down for awhile on a new filling until all the shapes meet together right? That's what it felt like in my mouth and I knew that something was happening to *my* teeth! I'd have to check it out when I got home or in the bathroom later. *Wow!*

While I was thinking about my teeth and playing my flute, the most incredible thing happened! There was this shriek from someone in the audience close to the stage, then another shriek, and then a couple more shouts came from other parts of the room. You had to be here to believe what was happening! Prophet Bryan called for the people that had just began to experience unusual miracles, besides the "glory rain," to come up on the stage to explain what had just happened to them. Five people came forward to give their accounts. Oh, my friend, wait until you hear what they said! This was so awesome!

One lady was jumping up and down and screaming and crying, "Oh my God, He is so *awesome*, my

Jesus is *so great!*" So Prophet Bryan gave her the microphone to start first.

"My husband left me five months ago alone with my two small children," she began. "I don't have any clue where he went off to. I've been a stay-at-home mom so I don't have a way to support myself and my kids yet. I had a little money tucked away but for the past three months I have had a very hard time being able to pay my bills and have been scraping to put food on the table for us. I've been praying everyday that my Jesus would supply all my needs from His storehouse of riches. Before the service started this morning, I prayed that God would please do a miracle in our finances."

"I was so overwhelmed," she continued, "when I saw the sparkly "rain" and I asked the Lord if there were financial miracles in the "glory dust". Immediately after I asked Him that question, I felt this big lump in my right front pocket that I *knew* was not there before. So, I stuck my hand into my pocket to see what it was and this is what I pulled out." When she finished talking, she burst into tears. Everyone cheered and clapped when they saw the miracle the Lord gave her.

Oh, *it was so sweet*, my friend. You've got to imagine this. She held up the biggest gold nugget I could ever imagine seeing in my life. *Not that I've really ever seen any before!* But this thing was as big as a *golf ball* and must be worth hundreds if not thousands of dollars!

"Thank you, Lord, for giving her such a mighty miraculous blessing!" Isn't that just *so awesome, friend?* How does that happen? Just out of the blue, a big gold nugget appears in her pocket! It's just like the "glory rain", just appearing out of nowhere.

Prophet Bryan looked over at me and smiled and motioned for me to continue playing my flute but more softly. "Keep praying! Oh, people, God is not finished yet. There is still much more He wants to do in this room today!"

Then turning back to the lady, he told her, "This is an extraordinary miracle! Our Jesus is so wonderful. What an awesome testimony of the extreme love and care our Heavenly Father has for His kids. I'll be interested to hear how much that nugget is worth. Be sure to get lots of pictures of it before you take it to get it converted to cash. That is definitely another miracle that we need to air on Cable TV News! Don't you all agree? Hallelujah!"

So, get this, friend! That woman was just the *first one to demonstrate what the Lord was doing!* There was more! When he had finished talking to her, three more people, a man and two ladies stepped forward to show evidence of their miracles. They put out their hands to show what the Lord had given them. Each of them had a very large, perfectly faceted gemstone in their hand. The man had a green stone like an emerald, one of the ladies had a beautiful blue gem like a sapphire and the other had a clear stone like a diamond. They were all so excited that the Lord had given them each a costly **jewel** stone!

The man was so overcome with emotion that he could barely talk. Finally he was able to compose himself and told us that his emerald stone had dropped down right by his right foot out of nowhere. He reached down to pick it up and immediately knew what the meaning of it was. He told us a story of how his grandfather had given his grandmother a beautiful emerald for their fortieth wedding anniversary. After he died and the family had to put her in a nursing home because she had gotten Alzheimer's disease, her children asked her about the emerald that he had given to her. She was never able to remember them or the emerald and the jewel was never recovered.

The man before us was so overwhelmed that the Lord had replaced the emerald with something so much larger and more extravagant than his grandfather was ever able to afford. He mentioned how wonderful it was that our God was in the business of restoration. He couldn't wait to take it home and show it to his family. There was hardly a dry eye in the place as everyone felt his emotion.

The lady holding out the sapphire said, with big tears dripped down her cheeks, that as she was standing by her chair worshipping the Lord, she heard a thump behind her and turned around to see what it was. There on her chair next to her Bible was this beautiful sapphire stone. She said she had recently lost a sapphire out of one of her ring settings but that this was many times larger than the stone she had misplaced. How the Lord wants to bless us more than we can even think or know. This was just so incredible that words just don't seem to be able to describe the awesomeness of the moment! Who could have imagined that this could happen at a little church like ours?

When it came time for her to share, the lady displaying the clear diamond stone said that the Lord had told her to look in her Bible at Exodus 28:18. When she picked up her Bible, the page immediately opened up to that verse, and there was this diamond-looking stone right on that page! She read the verse out loud to everyone and you won't believe what it says! It reads "And the second row shall be an emerald, a sapphire, and a diamond".

Oh, my Lord! Not only was it a verse that contained all three jewel stones that the three people had received, but it was also the "second" demonstration of miraculous gifts. What is the chance of that? And the types of stones were even in the order of the testimonies that were given. There was no chance involved in this miracle. These were strictly *divine appointments* and we all got to experience it right along with these people!

The place again exploded with the sound of clapping and screaming and praise to the Lord. Can you believe it? Not only had a gold nugget and mystery sparkle dust appeared out of mid-air but now these jewel stones. They were incredibly large and sparkly. I have never heard of anything like this before. Have you ever, my friend? What a supernatural day this was! How could there be anything more miraculous than this? This was so *supernatural* that it would have been hard to believe if it wasn't just happening before our very eyes. How could I keep playing my flute? I wanted to fall on my face before the Lord and just praise Him and weep for everything He was doing!

That big angel must be standing by me again giving me strength to keep standing and playing! I couldn't feel his presence so strongly this time but I just knew that he must be close by. Maybe somehow I was getting more used to this kind of miraculous power coming on me and going through me so that I was able to still keep standing and quietly play my flute.

What I really desired to do was let out a loud scream and jump up and down with joy and praise to the Lord! Many people were just exploding out of their seats and finding places to dance and jump up and down like they were bouncing on trampolines, similar to what I wanted to do! Many were expressing their excitement and emotions to the Lord without caring who was watching them or what anyone one else was thinking about them! There was so much freedom in this place!

12

So Amazing

The Lord is so good to us! How could He keep astonishing us with all these miracles? *It's all so extraordinarily unbelievable! There are just not enough words in the English language to describe the greatness of our Lord!* It's no wonder that He gave us a supernatural language to talk to Him with or we would never be able to express our gratitude for everything He does for us. I love You, Lord, so very much. Praise You and thank You!

I know some extraordinary portals to God's awesome glory and power were being opened wide this morning because the miracles were coming non-stop. I wonder if it is the Lord or the angels that open the portals to heaven. It makes me think of Jacob in the Bible when he saw the angels in his dream going up and down the ladder reaching into heaven. All I know is that the news media will have a very hard time believing all this and will think we have dreamed up a tall tale and are just making up all this stuff. I wish someone had invited the news media to come this morning and witness all this. Otherwise, the world will not want to believe all this, even though we know that it's true.

I know what I have seen and I know everyone else has seen the same thing in this place. Wait until they get on film those big jewels and the gold nugget and all the doctors' reports of the healings and the miracles of "glory dust" and new teeth fillings. I'm sure they will try to explain the "glory rain" away by saying that someone brought a container of glitter and was throwing or blowing it on the people.

But, they'll have a hard time trying to explain everything away like the way I've seen them do on some television shows. They say things like some weird phenomenon occurs when the atmosphere is charged with extra ions or some dumb thing like that. But for those who actually hear about this and believe with their hearts, they will be the ones the Lord will touch and draw to Himself. I pray that many people will be influenced into believing in our miraculous God who cares about all of us. I hope when they see all the miracles, they will know that He is a real God who is alive and desires to be a part of our lives.

How was it possible to be in so much of His Presence and still live to tell about it, I wondered? Prophet Bryan was gleaming with delight to see what the Lord was doing for His people. There was one last person left on the stage after the other four had shared their amazing miracles and gone back to their seats.

There was a young boy who was about 10 years old who was pacing back and forth like he couldn't wait to talk. He was rather pale and very thin and I couldn't tell if he was happy or sad because it was obvious that he had been crying for quite awhile. Prophet Bryan walked over towards him and waved his hand for the boy to come closer to him.

"Young man," Prophet Bryan spoke softly and gently to him and put a loving arm around his shoulder, "what did our Master Jesus do for you today?" With that, the young boy broke into sobs again and took a few moments to regain his composure before he was able to talk. I stopped playing my flute long enough to rush to the side of the stage to grab a handful of tissues and hurry back to hand them to him.

"That was my wheelchair over there," he said in a half sob, pointing to the right side aisle of the church where a wheelchair was sitting. "I have been in a wheelchair ever since I was old enough to sit up. I was born with the HIV virus, which was passed to me by my mother. She died four years ago of AIDS and I have been in the hospital most of my life being treated for AIDS, also. Dad and Mom back there adopted me," he said, pointing to a man and woman waving, who were in the same area where his chair was. "I don't know who my real dad is."

"When I saw the "glory rain" come down, I just got this great big burst of faith on the inside of me to believe that it was *my time to receive a miracle healing*. My adopted mom's sister was here on Friday night and she came straight over to our house after the meeting and started telling us all about the miracles that were happening here the other night. I think I started to believe for a miracle right then! So, when Mom and Dad agreed to come here this morning, I was so very happy. I've been waiting so patiently since Friday night for this morning to come! Thank you, Prophet Bryan for coming to our city."

"Oh, I have nothing to do with this. Jesus is the Miracle Worker!" the prophet exclaimed. "I just like to create an atmosphere and expectancy for Him to do His work. So please tell us more about what happened to you this morning."

"I began to feel strength come into my legs like I'd never felt before so I just knew that Jesus was starting to heal me at that very moment! That was when I decided to step down out of my wheelchair. Dad and Mom looked shocked at first at what I was trying to do but then they started helping me up to my feet and sure enough, I could stand. I took a step forward carefully, and then another and another and *each time I stepped forward, it got easier and easier! I have never been able to walk before but now I can! Look, the sores on my arms and legs are disappearing, too! I just know I am healed of AIDS right now!"*

With that, everyone in the place began screaming and cheering, crying and jumping for joy! The room was so loud, you could barely hear yourself *praise!* Can you believe it? I'm sure it's a day no one in this place will ever forget! After it quieted down a little, I continued to play my flute softly but it was really hard not being totally distracted by all that was happening. "Oh Lord, please give me strength. You are so *awesome!* Thank You for what you are doing for that boy and everyone in this place."

After the boy shared, Prophet Bryan broke down and sobbed. He hugged the boy for the longest time and then they both knelt down on the stage together. I began to think that now would have been an excellent time for the TV news cameras to be rolling. It was such a special, touching moment. If only the world could see how great our God is! All of a sudden, the "glory dust" completely covered both of them as they knelt there.

Prophet Bryan then motioned for me to come over closer to them and he pointed at my flute and then to the boy. I got from his motions that he was attempting to say, "play over this small boy while Jesus continues to minister to him", but since the Prophet was so overcome with emotion, he couldn't even get a word out. It was my complete honor to be asked to do such a thing. The young boy was totally blessing me with his story. Finally, Prophet Bryan got up to his feet to speak to the people in the audience. He hadn't even taught anything from the Bible yet because the Lord had other plans for the services, both Friday Night and this morning. I wondered if he would have time to speak at all this morning. My guess is that he would not, but maybe tonight.

He took the microphone and announced that the young boy's name was Steven and he hoped that Steven's family would be open to sharing his story for the world to hear. "Jesus is alive today and He is still the Healer." he exclaimed. "What an incredible God we have to serve."

The young boy wept on the stage in a crumpled heap on the floor as I played my flute over him. *Then I saw it!* Time seemed to stand still as I watched the miracle that was happening before my eyes. There was the huge angel again that I had seen on Friday night. I just knew the angel had been there all along but now my spiritual eyes were open to see him. He was standing beside me again only this time he had his hand lifted up over Steven.

I could see this brilliant radiance like liquid light coming down off of his hand and it was pouring down on Steven's head. Maybe it was like the holy fire that Moses saw when he experienced the burning bush that was not consumed. It was blue and white with a tiny speck of red-orange in the center. I wanted to scream and cry out for someone else to know what I saw but it was as if I was awestruck and frozen in place and all I could do was play my flute. The Lord had again opened up another extraordinary portal of power for me to see through. *It was all **so amazing!***

He must be strengthening Steven's body as he was doing for me and maybe he's burning out all the disease in Steven's fragile body so that the Holy Spirit could send new life in to replace all the bad diseased cells. The radiant fire could possibly be a physical demonstration of the glory that he receives from being in the Throne Room in the Presence of God.

Wow! This is so wonderful but fearfully awesome! I feel so privileged to get to witness this! There might not be anyone else in this whole room that sees what I'm seeing right now! Otherwise there would be a big stir from someone who *does* see him and the fire. I'm telling you, my friend; it is such a spectacular sight to see. I can relate to how Moses must have felt when he saw the burning bush. He was probably in total fear and awe.

He must be a ministering angel that ministers to Father's special family. All I know for sure is that he has ministered strength to *my* body. In fact, I'm sure he is strengthening me right now for me to be able to continue to stand and play my flute over this young boy. What a privilege this is to see such extraordinary things. What could be more *exciting* in life than experiencing all these supernatural miracles? Some people are really missing out, in my opinion. Ya know, I'm kind of curious if this awesome angel has a name. I'd be interested to know what to call him.

"You may call me *Strength*," came a voice into my ear. I looked up at the angel standing next to me, still holding his hand over the boy. He was looking back at me with a big smile on his face.

"You heard my thoughts?" I enquired of him in my mind without speaking it out and looking quite puzzled, I'm sure.

"I can hear your thoughts and your words," he replied back to me without moving his lips. "Jesus taught that your words have great power but in the spirit realm, your thoughts have power also. That's why Paul taught you in your Bible that you are to renew your mind. The enemy can use your thoughts as well as your spoken words. As spirit beings, we can all hear your thoughts as well as your words, according to what the Father allows."

"But how am I able to hear you talking to me." I inquired of this magnificent supernatural being.

"The God of the Universe has chosen to open a portal into the supernatural realms of heaven and has opened your spiritual eyes and ears *to see and hear into the spirit realm where I exist!* Otherwise, you would not have been able to see me right now let alone hear me. You have been chosen to assist the Prophet with your gifts. In order for you to even stand to play your instrument in this much of His Presence, your Heavenly Father had to send me to strengthen your body so that you are able to contain and withstand the power and presence of the Holy Spirit flowing through your body."

"You were right, that this young boy needs to be strengthened from the weakening and destruction that the evil disease caused in his body but it is different from the strength that your body needs. You are being taken through a purifying process in your soul and body so that the Holy Spirit can pour His breath through your spirit more and more. The more time you spend in the power and presence of the Spirit, the stronger your physical body will become to stand in the anointing. For now, I have been assigned to serve you as you assist the Prophet."

"Wow!" I thought, still playing my flute. "I am carrying on a conversation with you in my thoughts while I am still playing my flute over this boy. Is my flute having any effect on this boy if *you* are the one pouring supernatural strength back into him?" I asked Strength.

"Oh yes, my friend." he replied back to my mind as he smiled again. "You have no idea what an enormous gift you are giving to this young boy today. You are blowing the very breath of life and health upon him, as your Father breathed life into Adam and Jesus breathed eternal life upon His disciples. You have no small gift to give. You are blowing that instrument with the very same breath of the Holy Spirit as when He blew the mighty wind upon His people in the upper room of that most important Day of Pentecost."

"The Ancient of Days does not send me to just anyone unless there is a very important need. It was I who was sent to the Prophet Elijah in the wilderness as he sat under the juniper tree in order to strengthen him and it was also I and my assistants who were sent to Jesus in the wilderness to strengthen Him during His forty days of fasting. So you see that I would not have been sent to you unless the need was of great importance. You are very significant to the Father and His kingdom as is this Prophet you are assisting."

With that statement from the mighty angel, I felt my body sway as if I was about to fall out under the power of the Lord with the weight of the assignment the Lord had placed on my life. His holy angel "Strength" held out his strong arm to steady me from falling as he again filled my body with vitality and strength. I don't know how much time had passed for it seemed as if time had stood still while our "mind conversation" took place. The portal that had been opened to talk to Strength seemed to have closed because I no longer heard his thoughts talking to my mind anymore. "Darn, I spoiled my moment with Strength by thinking about my inadequacies!" I scolded myself under my breath. "I've got to walk in more confidence and faith! Thank You, Lord, for the great destiny You have planned for me!"

Prophet Bryan called Steven's parents up and asked them how they met this boy and how they came to adopt him. They told their touching story of how they had visited the Children's Ward at St. Joseph's Hospital and spotted this precious boy who seemed to have no family to love or care for him. His mother had been too ill to even visit him before her death. Their hearts went out to this young boy because he was so sweet and forgiving that they just couldn't help but fall in love with him.

I could see how they felt. I felt a very special closeness to him and I've never even met him before. He just seemed to have that way of melting your heart. It was a similar feeling to how close I felt to all those young people at the retreat I had just barely met, but this boy had a quality of tenderness that just made your heart be *so touched and drawn* to him.

I hope their family continues to come to our church after today. I'd like to get better acquainted with him. He seems to be much older and more mature for his age. He probably has had to grow up really fast to have to deal with all the pain and disease and death. But not anymore because today is a brand new day for him! Praise You, Jesus!

Prophet Bryan went over to Steven and helped him to his feet. "How do you feel, young man?" he asked him. "While Selima was playing the Holy Spirit's song over you, a mighty angel was also ministering strength to your body. Do you feel refreshed and strengthened now?"

So, Prophet Bryan had known that Strength was there too, then! I wonder if he saw Angel Strength pick me up on Friday night, too. I'll have to ask him some other time.

"Yes, I feel so great!" he shouted. *"I have never felt this good in my entire life!"* With that, he ran across the stage and leaped up into his adoptive father's arms and hugged and cried on his shoulder. Next, he hugged his mom for the longest time. Then, all of a sudden, he jumped off the stage and started running around the perimeter of the sanctuary leaping over people on the floor, weaving in and out of all the people and yelling *"I'm healed, I'm healed! Praise the Lord, I'm healed! It's a miracle! It's a sweet miracle!"*

At that moment, the place exploded. People were crying and laughing and shouting their praises to the Lord. Every kind of emotion and excitement was being displayed at that moment. It was so incredible! Like I had said earlier, now would have been another great opportunity for the TV cameras to be rolling!

13

Hidden Ones

What a special meeting this is! *The Lord is so good to us!* If only the whole world could know how great our God is and all the miracles He does for us. Soon they will get a glimpse of what He has been doing in this place when the TV station sends their team to come out to tape.

What an absolute privilege it was to talk to Strength! I hope the Lord allows me to talk to him again. He gave me some very interesting information. I wonder how long he will be assisting me. *What an incredible moment, so totally awesome! I can't wait to talk to Jason about our conversation!* But if I tell someone about our conversation, maybe I won't have access to that "portal" and he won't be able talk to me anymore. Maybe this is one of those secrets of the Lord that you just hold dear to your heart and *don't tell anyone.* I think our Lord wants us to have intimate secrets with Him that we can keep dear just between Him and us. For now, it will have to stay *our very special secret!*

"I love You so much, Lord! Thank You for sending Your Angel Strength to me to assist me. I feel so honored and humbled to be of service to You in playing my flute for You. It is such an awesome privilege that I can't begin to express how much it means to me!"

As I began expressing my heart to the Lord, the tears started to flow. I felt so close to my Lord, it was like He was wrapping His loving arms around me *and I felt so accepted!* Of course, there was hardly a dry eye in the place from Steven's story so I didn't mind that anybody could see the tears dripping down my cheeks. No one could have known that I had just had a conversation with an angel and that I was feeling hugged and loved on by the Lord Himself.

"Young man, young man, would you come up here, please!" Prophet Bryan called out, pointing into the crowd in the front of the pews. At first I couldn't see the person he was pointing to. But then, as he got closer, I saw who was coming up on the stage. It was my brother Jason! Oh, my Jesus! This *is* his day!

"The Lord has a word for you, young man." he continued. When Jason got to the stage he was grinning so big you would have thought he was the Cheshire cat in <u>Alice in Wonderland!</u> He quickly glanced over at me and gave me a quick "thumbs up" gesture. I couldn't wait to hear what the Lord was going to say to him through the Prophet.

"You have a very special call on your life, son." Prophet Bryan boldly announced. "The Lord has chosen to bless you and He is sending you to be a voice to the nations. You are to preach the Gospel of the Kingdom to your generation for the time is short. You will travel with another member of your family. Do you have a sister or brother here today?"

"Yes, she's my sister." he said smiling as he pointed at me still quietly playing my flute.

"Selima! I didn't know you had a brother but now the Word of the Lord is making everything perfectly clear. You both have a mighty call and anointing on your life and you are going to be launched out into a place where the miraculous signs and wonders of God shall be commonplace as He gives you the Message of the Kingdom to share with the youth of this world! Your generation is looking for the super-natural. The enemy has deceived the youth of this day with the great lie that the only supernatural they will ever encounter is from sorcery and the occult or the dark side. This reality is about to change, for God is about to reveal his **hidden ones** to the world and begin to demonstrate to the world that there is a *real* God; not a *counterfeit* God of *religion*, having a form of godliness but denying that the power of God is a reality for this generation."

"God is about to use the two of you in ways you would have never dreamed possible! You have already begun to see into the spirit realm more clearly, espe-cially you, Selima. You have experienced angels and have already had miraculous healings and miracles happen just by playing your flute. But our Father in Heaven is about to use you both in more unusual and different ways than you can even imagine right now.

You are about to let the world know that our Jesus is alive and He is a supernatural God who wants to see His family come home and be healed and set free. He has already demonstrated the unusual today, hallelujah. But, let me tell you, *there is so much more!"*

"Are your parents here today? Can they come up to the stage as well, please? By the way, son, what is your name?"

As our parents headed towards the platform, he answered the Prophet, "My name is Jason, Sir, and these are our parents, Jacob and Rachel."

"Jason, *Jason! Of course* your name is *Jason* which means *"healer"* for you shall go to the world to bring healing to *thousands of hearts, minds and bodies for Jesus' name sake!"*

"Jacob and Rachel are two very important names in our Old Testament Jewish heritage. Jacob was the grandson of our Forefather Abraham and one who was given the name Israel. Rachel was the one he loved so much that he worked fourteen years to receive her as his wife. It's very nice to meet you both. What are the chances of two people of the same name joining in marriage in our day as they did of old? I think there are no coincidences in this life."

"God planned it before time began that you two would marry and have a son and daughter that would impact their generation before the soon return of our Lord and Savior Jesus Christ of Nazareth, God's Son. Were you two aware of the great call that is on your youth? They are going to be a motivating force in the Kingdom of God and His favor and power rests heavily upon them."

"We were just talking briefly about that this morning on the way to Church," replied our dad. "They were really expecting the supernatural to occur this morning and I reminded them that God's Word says that He rewards that kind of faith and expectation of His visitation. They have really been pressing in to know the Lord in a greater way and experience everything He has for them so the Word of the Lord that you spoke over them today is very appropriate."

"That's incredible! You know, I asked your daughter the other night if she would pray about traveling with me and playing her flute at my meetings. I now know that I need to be asking for both your son and daughter to accompany me. There also seems to be one other young person in this audience who has a connection with these two who is also supposed to join them. That is, if you are going to give your permission, Mr. and Mrs. Jeruelli."

"Please, call me Jake. I couldn't be more thrilled than to see God demonstrate His mighty power in signs and wonders through my two kids. Are you two agreeable to this idea?" he inquired, looking over at Jason and me.

Jason burst out his answer towards Prophet Bryan, "*Yes, Sir,* I *definitely* want the *privilege* of traveling with you and I know Selima does too, because we have discussed it! Mom, is this okay with you?"

"Just like your dad, I'm thrilled and excited to see what the Lord has planned for the two of you," she replied. "Now, who was this other person you were talking about, Prophet Bryan?"

"Jason, Selima, do you know who the Lord may be referring to?"

"I'm pretty sure I know," I piped in. "Zoë Shepherd right down there on the front row, the pastor's daughter, is the one who lead me to the Lord. Ultimately our whole family has become members of the family of God because of her witness and knowledge of the Bible. She is my best friend and a good friend of Jason's, too."

"Miss Zoë! *Oh my, you are absolutely right, Selima!* Zoë, please come up here and join us." Zoë jumped up and ran to the stage and gave Jason and me a big hug and then stood between us.

"The Lord is calling you out as well!" Prophet Bryan continued. "I had a prophetic Word of the Lord for you earlier that I haven't yet given you. This has been such an eventful morning! I wasn't sure I was going to have time to deliver it to you until our meeting tonight."

"Zoë, you have a mighty call on your life as well! You are also destined to impact this generation with the anointing the Lord has placed on your life. He has given you a mighty gift for bringing His family members back home to Him. God shows me that He's gifted you with such a simple but thorough presentation of the gospel and God's Word says that "he who wins souls is wise". He has given you wisdom much beyond your years in order to bring the youth to know the Lord in this final hour before His soon return!"

"It is no accident that your name is Zoë Shepherd. Zoë is the Greek word for *life and a shepherd is a guide and leader of sheep – that is – God's sheep – His family.* You shall bring many people to *eternal life* in the Lord and give them special guidance as it seems you have already done for this Jeruelli family. What a threesome you shall be. You know, I just love the youth and I would love to mentor these three in the ways the Lord has taught me. Pastor John and Debra, what do you think of all this? Please come and join all of us up here."

"I am just *overwhelmed and speechless* and that is hard to say, coming from me!" Pastor John exclaimed when he and his beautiful wife, also a redhead, reached the stage and took another mike to speak into.

"I am so overcome with emotions! This is all so incredible; please tell me this isn't a dream. The whole service has been so astounding; there are just no words great enough to express it. Last Friday night and today have been the most supernatural and spectacular services I have ever been in. We definitely need to get the TV news station in here and broadcast to the world how great our God is."

"Can you believe this day? We've had "glory rain" fall, a huge gold nugget appear, jewels appear, the visitation of angels and the young boy getting healed of AIDS. And now our young people have been commissioned by the Lord. What more can we ask for or even imagine? This has been too much to take in all at once, who would agree? And this is after all the healings and miracles that we saw take place on Friday night! Oh, Church, are you excited about what our God is doing in this very place?"

With that inquiry, the place exploded in praise and joyful celebration again. The room was deafening; it was so loud. No ballgame has anything on us, that's for sure! But, when he named off all the miracles, he didn't know about the miracle of my conversation with the angel Strength or his touching Steven with fire. I wonder if I am the only one who saw that, probably Prophet Bryan did also. I know he saw Strength on Friday night and this morning but did he actually see the *fire, I wonder*? In both services, the angel did *miraculous* things that only maybe one or two know about. Maybe I should be telling my story on TV, too. But, no, on second thought, I don't want to do anything that would cause the Lord to not want to send him back to assist me again. Secrets with the Lord are sometimes just too intimate to share!

When it calmed down a bit, Pastor John continued, "I am totally elated to have my daughter involved in your meetings, Prophet Bryan. If they are anything like the services we have just had today and Friday, then the world will be turned upside down in *no* time!"

"I would feel *quite honored* for Zoë to join these two godly Jeruelli kids. They are *treasures!* Our God is on the move and He is looking for people who will follow Him and demonstrate His love as He did while He was on this earth and all three of these youth certainly qualify in my book."

"Oh Church, are you ready to send out our first youth ambassadors? We will have to discuss the possibility of hiring a tutor for them to continue their schooling when they are traveling to other places, but getting the Gospel of the Kingdom out to their generation is of equal if not more importance to our Lord than their schooling. This has been all quite amazing! Let's sing one more song and dismiss the service and we will meet back here at 6:00 this evening. What shall we expect of the Lord tonight? I don't know but I'm sure it will probably be "above and beyond all we could ask or think" as He has done in these two meetings. Take it away, music team."

I quickly whispered to Zoë that we needed to talk and she suggested riding over to our house with us, staying for the afternoon and riding back to church with us tonight. I said that would be perfect and told her to go ask.

I quickly picked up my flute to my lips and joined the team in the last song of the service. This weekend has been something extraordinary and it's not over yet. I can't wait to talk to Zoë since we have so much to talk about! Oh Dear Lord, You are so good to us! I will be *so* careful to keep my conversation with Strength a secret!

14

Supernaturally Transformed

As soon as we climbed into the back of our SUV, Zoë gasped as she looked at Jason and me. "Selima, Jason, you guys are *covered* in "glory dust"! It's all over your face and arms and clothes. It's so fine but so sparkly. I'm guessing it's all over your flute, too.

"Oh, you don't even know! It's all over my flute and on the inside of my case, *which was closed up during the meeting*, by the way! It was all over my hands so while I was trying to clean it off, I kept putting more back on my flute and it doesn't wipe away very easily either. But, it's such an incredibly miraculous material. I wonder if it was tested, if it would be worth something at a precious metals' shop or something. *I'm sure that gold nugget we saw earlier will be pretty valuable!* Speaking of the miraculous material, the fillings in my teeth were feeling kind of different in the service this morning. Can you see anything different or unusual about them?" I opened my mouth wide for Zoë to look inside.

"Oh, Dear Jesus! They are so shiny, Selima! Look at her fillings, Jason!"

"Wow, they are really shiny! I'm pretty sure God did something miraculous to your fillings, Lima. They don't look like they used to."

"I'll look at them in the bathroom mirror when we get home. We're almost there. What about you two, did any of your amalgam fillings change?

"It didn't even occur to me to look." Zoë exclaimed. What do you think, guys? Are they shiny?" she asked and then gave them the wide-opened mouth pose to show two very shiny teeth fillings.

"They are, *they are*, Zoë!" I gasped. "They are a silvery-gold looking color and very shiny. Jason, it's your turn." Jason opened wide and sure enough, he had two shiny silvery looking fillings, too. Are my fillings gold or silver or maybe that color is platinum?"

"Yours are a very silvery color. It very well could be platinum, though. It would be just like our God to put the most valuable of all the metals in our teeth." Zoë suggested.

"We're home! Hurry, I want to go look at my teeth in the big mirror! Come on, let's all go check it out. Oh, you guys, this has been the best three days of my life!" I exclaimed. "I thought the retreat weekend was amazing but this has been *something else again!"*

"Come on! Let's go up to the upstairs bathroom where the big mirror and row of bright lights are so we can all see at once. I'm excited to see my new fillings. I just can hardly *believe it!* It sounds like if we start traveling with Prophet Bryan that this kind of thing could be an *everyday occurrence!*"

"Oh yeah, *I know what you mean, Selima!*" Zoë exclaimed. "Since the meeting on Friday, I feel like I have been floating on *'Cloud Nine'!* I can hardly believe this is *happening! Look, it's true! They are really shiny! What a miracle God gave us without us hardly even noticing!*"

"Selima, you didn't tell me that Prophet Bryan had invited you to go with him to play at his meetings. Of course we haven't really talked since Friday night when all this started happening. And it was even more incredible for him to include *all of us! Thank you, by the way,* for suggesting that it was possibly *me* that the Lord was referring to, when there was supposed to be someone else to join you guys. It's going to be such a fantastic adventure!"

"You know, he travels all over the world! Africa, South America and the Holy Land are the ones I know for sure. That is just going to be *so exciting!* I wonder if he is going to take us to foreign countries with him. We might have to get passports and shots and all that kind of stuff. Oh, I hate getting shots."

"You aren't the *only* one!" I agreed. I don't know anyone that is very fond of getting shots, *ya know?* Come on, you two. Let's go to my room and talk. I think Mom is making some sandwiches for lunch. We should probably be down there helping her out. I'm sure she understands, though, that we have a lot to talk about."

"Zoë, I've *got* to talk to you about Friday night and yesterday. Listen to this; *I shook all night long and all morning up until early yesterday afternoon!* My understanding is that it's because the power of God is going through my body so strongly when I play the flute that it can hardly contain it. I think it must be like when you get electrocuted, you can shake violently. *(I wasn't about to tell them that an angel named* Strength *had told me that and that he was sent there by the Lord to assist me!)*"

"But also, yesterday morning, I was laughing so hard for the longest time and I couldn't even stop myself. I would think I was about to stop but then, it would start right back up again. It was like someone else was laughing in my belly and *I was just going along for the ride!*"

"*Oh yeah, that's called "holy laughter"!* Zoë screamed out, "and it only happens when the Spirit of God fills your belly with joy. That has only happened to me *once! Wow,* **Sweet**, *Selima! Everything is happening to you!*"

"But, Zoë, I haven't even told you the whole story yet. You know Friday night when Prophet Bryan gave me that Word from the Lord after he talked about my name? I fell down in the power of the Spirit, but did you notice how soon after I fell that I got right back up again and then he told me to continue to play my flute?" Zoë nodded with curiosity in her eyes and so I continued. "I have had a *really big angel* standing next to me in both meetings and he has been giving me strength to stand up in the "glory" and he's been infusing me with some kind of heavenly air to breathe so I can play my flute. *That big angel picked me up and put me back on my feet!"* I shouted. (I hoped I hadn't revealed too much by telling both of them that, but I knew they were my secret-keepers so I felt safe to at least tell them that.)

"There's no way that anything like that could happen, Selima, no way!" Zoë yelled back.

"Totally, I am so serious! Not only that, but you know when Steven was kneeling on the stage this morning and I was playing over him with my flute? That big angel had his hand up over Steven's head and I saw this stream of light like liquid fire coming out of his hand and landing on Steven's head. I don't know if I was the only one to get to see it but it *was so extraordinary and supernatural!* It's possible that Prophet Bryan saw it but I don't know until I talk to him about it."

(Oh, great, now I've done it! I'm not sure if maybe *that* was the Lord's secret too, but I hope He understands that I want to tell my closest confidantes about His supernatural wonders, especially if we are going to be traveling together with the Prophet. Lord, please forgive me if it was wrong for me to tell them that much.)

"Selima, God is really *opening* your eyes to see into the spirit realm, *big time!* That is just too incredible! I didn't see that and I'm sure if others had seen it, they would have been screaming for everyone else to look. How in the world did you keep from just exploding and yelling it out to *everyone in the place!* Do your mom and dad know?"

I shook my head no and she kept on. "That angel must really trust you to keep his presence unknown. What does he look like, Selima?"

"He's very large and tall, maybe close to seven foot or taller, I'm not sure. He's really strong and muscular and he has quite dark bronze-looking skin. I never saw any wings or anything like that. He just looks like a very large man."

"Wow, that is just so awesome, Selima!" she exclaimed and then continued, "Friday night I *did* hear the angels singing and playing instruments. That was the most beautiful sound. We are being given so many blessings we can barely contain them all! It's so *overwhelming* to have all these *supernatural experiences!* Just wait until the Cable News Station starts broadcasting what is going on in our humble little church. We will *hardly* be able to get a seat in our *own church!* People will be coming from all over wanting to be a part of what is happening with us."

"I can't tell if it's just when Prophet Bryan is present or whether God is really changing things in our church, though." Zoë continued. "My parents have been talking about Friday night nonstop. God is getting us ready for the really big things He is going to show us in the very near future. I just know it is getting to the end of this age, as we know it. We just *have to be ready for so much more*, whatever that is."

"It is time for the young people to stop spending all their time on *video games and movies* and begin experiencing the *real thing for themselves!*" Zoë continued. *"Do you know what I mean?* What kind of life could be more exciting than *this?* It's one thing to earn jewels or gold nuggets at the end of a level of some kind of virtual reality or video game, but to *have it actually appear for real- out of thin air is quite another thing altogether, ya know?* Encountering some kind of mystical creature on a video game that someone made up in their imagination is not even *close* to having *an angel actually pick you up and set you back on your feet for real! Oh, I can't even fathom it! Are we dreaming here or is this really happening to us?"*

"No wonder you were shaking all night and day and then getting that *"holy laughter"! That right there is a miracle!* You can't shake for that length of time without it being *supernatural!* And having Holy Spirit laugh through you with His joy is quite another miracle. What do you suppose is going to happen *tonight?"*

"Wow, thank you, Ms. Debra. Those sandwiches look great!" Zoë greeted our mom as she entered the room with a tray full of sandwiches, chips and grapes. "We were going to come and help you. Sorry we never made it back down there. We have just been so engrossed in our conversation that we didn't even notice how the time has flown by."

"Don't mention it!" Mom smiled. "I know you three have a lot to talk about. Please, just enjoy. These are exciting days, aren't they?"

"They definitely are, Ms. Debra! Thanks again for the lunch. It sure looks delicious." Zoë called after our mom as she headed back downstairs. "That sure was nice of her to be so thoughtful."

"Thanks, Mom! Sorry we didn't give you any help! Mom, guess what?! We all have **supernaturally transformed** *fillings in our teeth!"* I called after her as she had already gotten halfway down the stairs.

"You have what? Did I hear you right, you all have changed fillings?" she exclaimed as she rushed back upstairs into my room.

"Yah, Mom, look!" I opened my mouth wide and Zoë and Jason followed suit. Everyone's fillings were a new, very shiny color as we looked at each other with opened mouths.

"They sure are! This is a miracle we can *document, kids!* We'll have to take you to the dentist and share the miracle with him and he will be able to verify that they *never* looked like *this before!* I'll tell your dad. I'm sure he will be excited about it, too. Have a nice lunch." With that, she left the room.

"Thanks again, Mom." I called. "Speaking of the three of us having a lot to talk about, Jason, you have been extremely quiet over there on my bean bag chair. Come over and have some lunch. What do you have to say about all of this?"

15

Out of Nowhere

J ason was silent for so long that I thought at first that he hadn't even heard my question. He was motionless with a faraway gaze. Finally, he got up and came over to the tray of food and grabbed a sandwich, a handful of chips and a napkin. Then he plopped himself down at the end of my bed on the opposite side from where Zoë was sitting cross-legged. I was sitting at the head of my bed with a couple of pillows propped up behind me.

"I guess I'd have to say that I'm just *speechless* and *awestruck!*" he finally muttered. "It is almost too much to take in, all in such a short length of time. I've been thinking about what you two have been saying but also what Prophet Bryan said to me, and also to all of us together. Can you believe that we all have names that mean something to our lives?"

"I've been wondering what my friends are going to say. Micah is not really that into spiritual things, but just wait until he hears about *all of this!* I'll bet he'll be more interested after I tell him what happened today. When he hears that we're going to have the Cable TV News come out and record what is going on, he'll be asking some questions."

"It would be so *cool* if he started coming to church more often. Not that church is where it's at. A personal relationship with our Lord is where it's at. Without a close relationship, going to church is nothing more than a religious act and *who needs religion?* Our God is gathering His family into His Kingdom and He didn't intend for us to mess everything up and make serving Him be about a bunch of do's and don'ts that don't mean anything."

"Oh, you are so right, brother!" I exclaimed. "Prophet Bryan sure gave you a clear word from the Lord. You've got *something to say* to our generation. They need to hear about a *real* relationship with the Lord and see some dynamite power being displayed. Get rid of all the stupid rules that religion puts on us and let's have some real miraculous Holy Spirit signs and wonders to demonstrate that His power and presence is with us. Our Lord is alive and wanting the world to know His power is in us, His body."

Jason continued, *"Yah,* when I tell my friends that I have *supernatural fillings* and had sparkly dust come out of mid-air and land on me, they are going to think *I have totally lost it!* It's all so bizarre but also completely awesome to think that we are just little "nobody's" in this world but yet He is doing these incredible things to us and through us."

"Oh, my Lord, check this out! My hands are covered with that sparkly "glory dust" again! It looks like it is coming out of my pores! My palms are covered! The backs are covered, too! I know all this wasn't here a while ago, because I washed my hands when we were in the bathroom looking at our teeth."

"Wow, this is *too much!* We are not even in church or worshipping the Lord or doing *anything* related to church other than discussing how He's blessing us. Does this mean that we can have *this "glory dust" appear to us just anywhere or anytime?"*

"Oh, Dear Jesus, I have it too!" cried Zoë. "Look, my hands look like I dipped them in glitter and I have also washed my hands before we left Church! *Sweet!* This must be a sign that the Lord wants to do the supernatural in our lives *all the time*, not just in a church building or someplace like that."

"You know, this is the *perfect* thing to introduce people to our Jesus. Just ask someone if they want to see a miracle before their eyes, and then hold out your hands and watch the Lord bring "glory dust" right out of your pores. I think He is just waiting for some everyday "nobody's" with innocent childlike faith to expect Him to do the miraculous and then He will meet their expectations right then and there."

"Even better yet," Jason interjected, "maybe the Lord will use *us* to demonstrate how the miracles can happen to *someone else!* We could tell them to hold out *their* hands and He could bring "glory dust" out of *their* pores! *That* would sure get their attention! At least, long enough to tell them about our Sweet

Jesus and that He loves them and wants *them* in His heavenly family."

"Can you imagine all the possibilities of this phenomenon happening just anywhere? He wasn't singling anyone out at church today. Whoever happened to be up at the front when the "rain" was falling out of mid-air got to *enjoy* it, and also all those who ran forward to get in on it, all received the same miracle."

"Okay, tell it, Big Brother!" I chimed in. *"My hands are sparkling, too! This is the most amazing phenomenon!* I have never heard of this before. Zoë, *you're* the *"PK"* here, "preacher's kid", *have you ever heard of this before?"*

"Not before today, Sis! We'll have to ask Prophet Bryan how long *he* has known about it, since he knew enough to call it *'glory dust'"*.

"*Well!*" I exclaimed. "We have seen "glory dust" fall out of thin air at church, and we have seen it come out of our pores. I wonder if it will also appear on other things like Bibles or furniture or other stuff like that. I'm going to take a search of this room. We've been talking about it enough and the Lord is here listening to our conversation or we wouldn't have it all over our hands. I believe He can meet our expectations again and show us a sign right here in this *very* room. *Let's take a closer look!*"

No sooner had I said that when Zoë let out a loud squeal. *"Selima, look right here on your dresser! There is sparkling dust everywhere! This is so absolutely amazing!"*

Next, it was Jason's turn to be completely surprised and amazed. *"You guys! Look in my shoes over here by the beanbag where I took them off! They are covered inside and out! My feet were just in them a little while ago, so how did the dust get inside unless it has happened just since we have been talking about it?"*

Now it was my turn to be wowed. *Not only were his shoes covered, but my shoes inside my closet were covered, inside and out!* God was meeting and exceeding our expectations. My clothes hanging in the closet had sparkles on them. Everywhere I looked had a fine sparkly substance dusted on it as if the Lord had blown it all over the room. The more we looked, the more there was. It seemed to be multiplying before our **VERY** eyes!

"Mom, Dad, come quickly! You've got to see this!" I screamed at the top of my voice. This was all too spectacular to figure out. I got down on my knees to praise and worship my Lord for the awesome and wonderful miracle He was doing in my bedroom. The Spirit filled my insides and I began to laugh and laugh, louder and louder. Pretty soon, Zoë broke out in uncontrollable laughter and then Jason. We were all laughing too hard to talk when Mom and Dad walked in.

"What's going on in here?" they both yelled in unison. *"Oh, My Lord and God! The "glory rain" has been falling in your room!"* Dad exclaimed. *"It is everywhere!"*

With that, they both looked at each other and then broke out in the "spirit of laughter" also, and everyone was laughing uncontrollably. I have never heard my dad laugh so hard and so loud. Mom fell over onto the bed and was just laughing like I have never heard her laugh before.

Jason fell back onto the beanbag and was rolling back and forth on it, laughing and laughing. The beanbag had also gotten covered with the dust so now he was rolling in the sparkly dust. Everything and everyone was now covered with this unusual "glory dust" that God had supernaturally poured out into my room.

This was *so supernatural!* Who could have imagined that sparkly "glory dust" could just appear *out of nowhere* and be all over your bedroom, on clothes and shoes, furniture, anything and everything? We must have opened up another mighty portal of God's divine power and favor. Who was I to have this happen to me, in my room? I'm nobody special. I'm going to look in Jason's room. I'm sure that the Lord must have put "glory dust" in his room as well.

When the laughing had subsided somewhat, I announced "Come on, everyone! Let's go look in Jay's room. I'm guessing that this is happening in there as well." As we entered the room, there it was, everywhere. "*Oh, look, it's everywhere! It IS in here, too!* What do you suppose this means, Dad? We've never had this happen until today at church. Now it's in our house."

"I don't know, Selima. I know that all the articles in the tabernacle and the temple in the Bible were either solid or overlaid with gold and some with silver. Maybe it's a sign of God's purification or a setting apart for God's service. Just as those items in the temple were for God's service, maybe this is also a sign of His covering and purification for service. But, who am I to say? It's just a guess. I know that all three of you were told in the meeting today that you were being set apart for His service and sent out to proclaim the Gospel of Kingdom of our Lord. Maybe if Zoë was at home right now, her bedroom would be covered with the same miracle substance. We should call your folks, Zoë, and ask them about this. Where did Prophet Bryan go after the service today, does anyone know?"

"He went home with my family," Zoë replied. "I'll call over there and see what's happening and ask about this miraculous sign. Maybe Prophet Bryan knows more about this. This is sure pretty *awesome* and so completely *unusual!* I wonder if other people that were in church today are experiencing this, too."

Let me just pause for just a moment to speak to you, my friend. I know this sounds kind of strange, but you should look at the palms of your hands right now. I believe that God wants *you* to experience His supernatural miracles as well and that He wants to meet *your* expectations too, like He is doing with us.

So, go ahead! Get under a bright light or sunlight and roll the palms of your hands around so that the pores catch the light and you may see God's "glory dust" on you as well. Watch as God gives you a miracle *right now at this very moment!* The "glory dust" will be the size of the pores on your hands.

When you *do* see some tiny sparkles, go tell someone else about it. It multiplies as you tell others about it, so give it away. It may even appear in your room like it has in ours. *Expect a miracle!* God is waiting for you to expect His supernatural power to be displayed in your life, too. Open a "portal of supernatural power" of your own. Oh, and by the way, be sure and check your fillings if you have amalgam in your mouth. You just might find that they have turned very shiny like ours. Keep checking for both things every day this week and be amazed at what the Lord is going to do for you!

After Zoë made her phone call to her house, she came back jumping up and down and was so excited we could barely get her to talk. *"What is happening, Zoë?"* I pleaded. *"We want to know, too! Is the "glory dust" in your bedroom, too?* Did you talk to Prophet Bryan about this?"

"Oh, Selima!" she exclaimed. "It is just too unusual for words. I don't know what to think or feel. When I called home, my dad answered, and when I started to tell him what was happening, I heard this gasp and a loud thump. I just sensed that he must have immediately fallen down in the power of the Lord."

"Then, Mom came over and took the phone from him and when I started telling her what was going on, I heard a loud noise and then she was gone, too. Next, David came over to the phone, insisting that I tell him what was going on and what was so horrible that caused Mom and Dad to faint. Of course they hadn't fainted but he wasn't aware of that, yet."

"When I began to tell him what was happening over here, I heard a loud "OOOHHH" and then he was gone. I'm sure Becky didn't know whether to answer the phone or not so she yelled towards the phone *"Who is that on the phone?"* and I yelled back that it was I. She yelled out for Prophet Bryan and that was the last I heard of her voice."

"Oh wow, I can't believe all this! Maybe there is so much glory going through the phone lines that while I'm talking to someone on the other end, they are just falling out in the power of God. Or the Lord has filled our house with His presence like He has here. That's all I can figure. We have certainly entered into a new realm of power and glory in the Lord today! The world is so ready to see the church come alive and offer something that is extraordinary like our supernatural God is. When that happens is when the world will take notice of what we have to say. The church has been so lifeless that hardly anything that we do or say draws the world to the Lord. So I don't know if my room has "glory dust" or not but I'm guessing it probably does. We are experiencing so much *amazing glory* right now, that I'm curious why we haven't gotten "slain in the spirit" ourselves!"

When Zoë made that comment, I began to ponder if maybe Strength had come to our house and was strengthening our bodies so that we weren't falling down in the power. I guess it's certainly possible. But why would it be important for the Lord to desire us to be able to stand, I wonder? Maybe He's training our bodies to get used to the "glory" and still be able to stand up in it. That must have been Holy Spirit answering my question while I was still asking it. I wouldn't have thought of that myself. Yeah, that makes a lot of sense. When we travel with Prophet Bryan, we won't be of much use to him if we are falling down on the floor with everyone else.

"So anyway," Zoë continued, "I waited for a while for Prophet Bryan to answer the phone but he must have not been in the same room with them so he probably didn't hear Becky's call. I finally decided just to hang up after waiting for a little while."

"I wonder when they will come out of being "drunk in the spirit" so that they can call us back. I'll be really curious to hear what Prophet Bryan's reaction will be when he comes into the room and sees all of them in a heap on the floor. He's not going to know what to think or how it happened. Maybe I had better call over there again and see if he will answer. They might have not hung up the phone if they are all still 'slain in the spirit'."

Zoë got up and called over to her house again but there was only a busy signal indicating that they hadn't hung up the phone yet. "Still busy!" she exclaimed. "Wow! They must really be "out in the spirit". I wonder if Prophet Bryan has even come in the room yet. What if he is now "slain in the spirit", too? *What do you think is happening over there? I'm curious to know if they are all covered with the "glory dust", too!"*

"I guess the only way to know anything about what's going on over at your house now would be to drive over there to see." I interjected. "What if they don't come out of their "spiritual stupor" before the service starts tonight? *We had better drive over there now! What is the Lord doing with all of us today? It's been all so supernatural and extraordinary, almost too much to handle for one day! I can totally relate to what Jason said earlier! I'm totally speechless and awestruck, too! Let's get going!*

"Dad, is it possible for you to drive us over to Zoë's house, please? We need to talk to Prophet Bryan before the service tonight about what's been going on over here and see what's happening with her family over there since they aren't answering the phone."

"I'd be happy to take you." Jacob replied as he smiled at me and put his arm around my shoulder in a loving gesture. "Let's be going then. I'm pretty curious about what's going on over there myself! Who's all going?"

"I'm coming along, too!" Jason piped in. "So I guess that makes it the four of us, including Zoë, Lima and you, Dad. I can hardly wait to get there. What are we going to find there, do you think?"

"Wait up! I want to join you guys too," yelled out our mom from the bedroom. *"I'll be right there!"*

"HURRY, LET'S GO!"

To be continued …..

Other Books Recommended by the Author

By Ruth Ward Heflin
>River Glory
>Revival Glory
>Golden Glory
>Harvest Glory

By David Herzog
>Desperate for New Wine
>Mysteries of the Glory
>Glory Invasion

By Bob Shattles
>Revival Fire and Glory
>Souls Harvest

Printed in the United States
205735BV00001B/1-186/P